Marionettes
How to Make and Work Them

by
HELEN FLING

Illustrated by Charles Forbell

Dover Publications, Inc.
New York

Published in Canada by General Publishing Company, Ltd., 30 Lesmill Road, Don Mills, Toronto,
Ontario.
Published in the United Kingdom by Constable
and Company, Ltd.

This Dover edition, first published in 1973 is
a revised republication of the work originally published in four volumes under the title *Marionette
Hobby-Craft*. This edition contains a new table of
contents.

International Standard Book Number: 0-486-22909-2
Library of Congress Catalog Card Number: 72-95675

Manufactured in the United States of America
Dover Publications, Inc.
180 Varick Street
New York, N. Y. 10014

CONTENTS

MAKING MARIONETTE AND PUPPET HEADS

MAKING MARIONETTE HANDS, FEET, LEGS, ARMS AND BODIES

STRINGING AND MANIPULATING MARIONETTES

PRODUCTION AND STAGECRAFT

Making
Marionette and
Puppet Heads

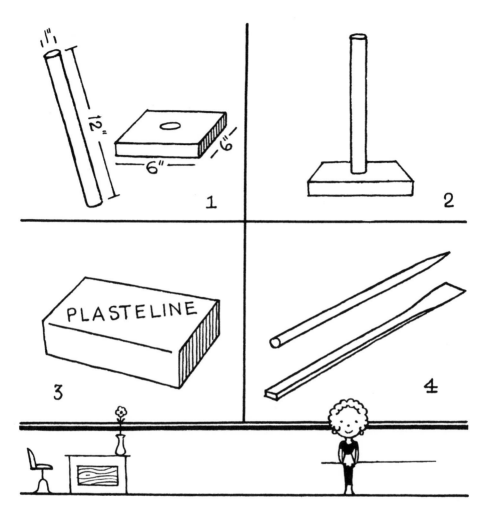

Note. First make an armature.

1. 1½ inch dowel sticks for upright of armature. Bore 1½ inch hole in center of block of wood 6 inches square.

2. Armature completed, ready for modeling.

3. Procure a pound block of plasteline which is most practical for all purposes of modeling.

4. Whittle a couple of sticks shaped like above for modeling tools.

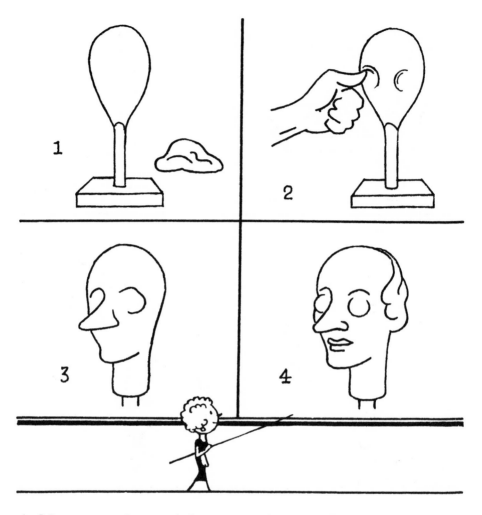

1. Mount on and around dowel stick the plasteline in general shape of an egg and about the size of a 3½ inch head minus the neck.

2. Begin by using thumbs, pressing in to make eye sockets.

3. Add portions as required for nose, chin, neck, brows, etc.

4. Refine lips, eyes and general shape of head, remembering bone structure underneath.

Note. Ears are not necessary if hair or hat will cover, unless needed for characterization.

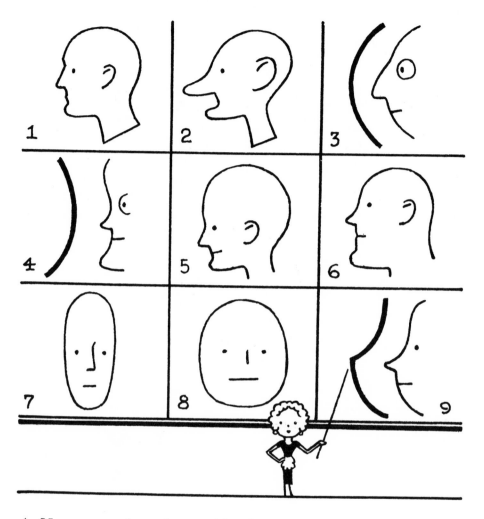

1. Note proportions of normal head.

2. Note exaggerations of features with same relative proportions.

3. Convex profile denotes action.

4. Concave profile denotes patience.

5. Large top head denotes mental type.

6. Large lower head denotes physical type.

7. Long narrow head, easy going.

8. Wide head, combative.

9. Combination profile, plodding.

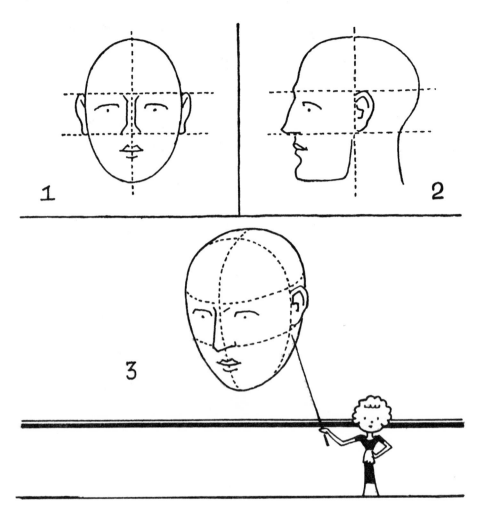

1. Note dimensions—nose 1/3 of head.

2. Note ear and nose position—ear center of head balance.

3. Perspective of 1 and 2.

Note. Most beginners fail to have forehead and back head development to models. The proportions of the normal head should be followed closely as a basis to work from in character exaggerations.

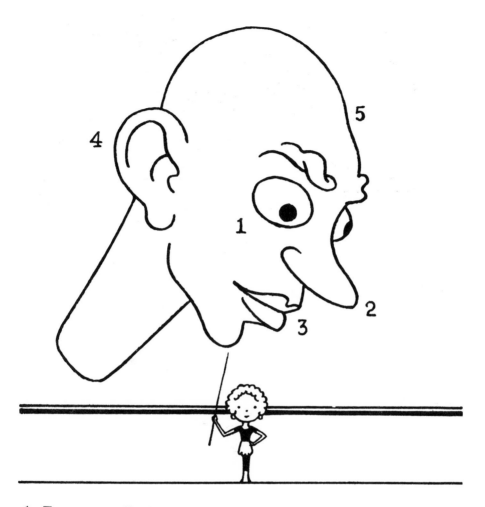

1. Eyes generally larger than normal except when necessary for squints and frowns, according to character wanted.

2. Get much character in nose.

3. Important feature to work out.

4. Make ears large.

5. Give feeling of bone structure of head.

Note. All features generally exaggerated as in cartoons, avoiding undercuts.

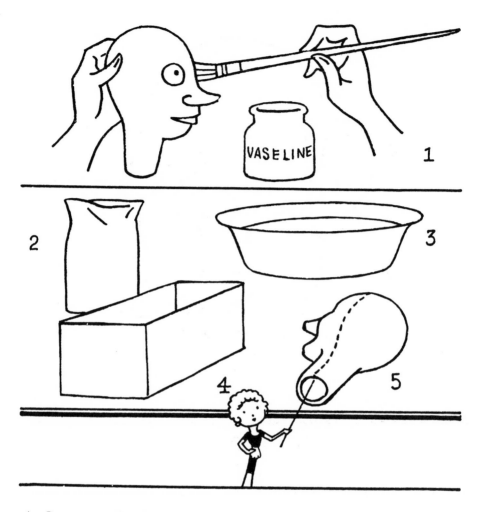

1. Coat entire head with thin layer of vaseline.

2. Have ready 1 pint of plaster of paris.

3. Bowl or pan 1 qt. size 2/3 filled with cold water.

4. A cardboard box 4 inches wide, 6 inches long and 4 inches high.

5. Draw line all around head with stick to divide front half from

   back, and place gently inside so as not to disturb or mar the shape.

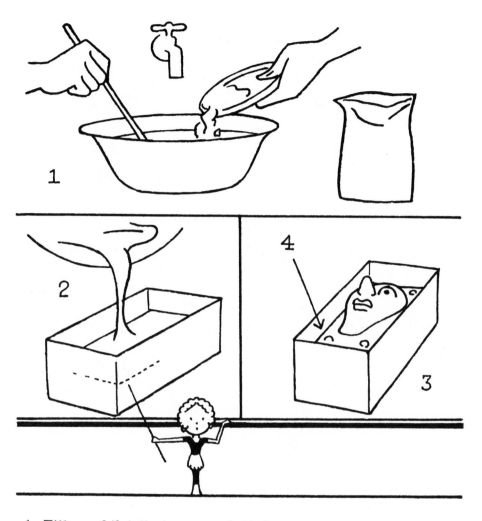

1. Fill pan 2/3 full of water and sift 3 cups of plaster of paris slowly into the pan of water, and when it stops bubbling, stir until it is of the consistency of very thick cream.

2. Fill box half full of the mixture.

3. Deposit head in mixture, face up, until submerged to guide line around head. Leave undisturbed until mixture hardens.

4. Put vaseline coated marbles half submerged in each corner to become register locks.

1. Shows method of placing head sidewise to avoid undercuts in case of long nose, pointed chin, etc.

2. In this case draw lines around head from forehead down nose to chin and back of head.

3. After coating surface of hardened plaster with vaseline, fill up rest of box with more plaster of paris mixture. If nose should protrude, pile extra mixture to cover completely with about ½ inch to spare.

4. When all is set and hard, tear off outside of box.

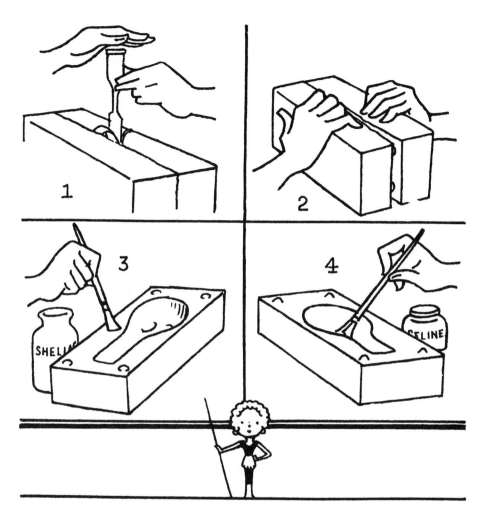

Note. Cast will get warm in the process. When cool, it is set.

1. Gently tap and pry open with chisel or kitchen knife, placing small damp piece of cardboard used as wedge.

2. Pull parts apart and take plasteline head out. (Save plasteline to make other heads later.)

3. Shellac inside of cast to preserve.

4. When dry, coat with thin layer of vaseline.

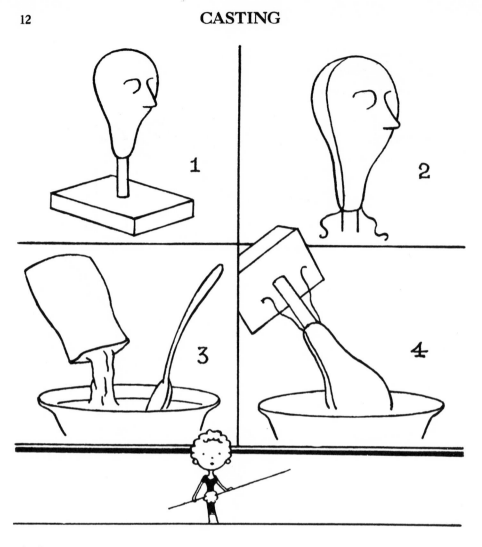

1. Have ready your modeled head in plasteline.

2. Place heavy thread all around your model, dividing the head in half, being careful that the thread is pressed into the model, leaving the two ends of the thread exposed and free.

3. Mix plaster of paris mixture to the consistency of cream.

4. Dip the model carefully into the mixture so that all parts of the model are covered without disturbing the thread.

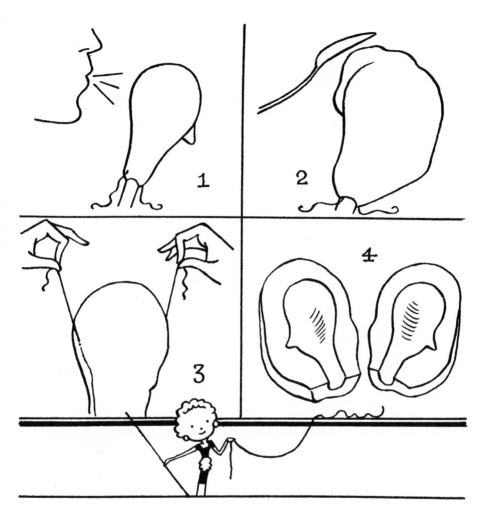

1. Blow on the head to distribute the mixture into all crevices. This is to prevent bubbles and air holes from forming. Repeat this process.

2. As soon as the mixture is a little thicker, begin to pile it over the model until the covering is two or three inches over all.

3. When the cast has become firm, but before completely hardening, grasp both ends of the thread and pull upwards carefully.

4. This will cut the cast and divide it into two halves, when it is ready for the paper-mache or the plastic wood process.

1. Have ready plastic wood, water and your thumbs.

2. Press plastic wood firmly into cast so as to fill every crevice and wrinkle, first moulding a plastic wood shape or pancake with wet hands. This prevents sticking. Head will be hollow.

3. When putting plastic wood in cast, allow a little to be built above the top surface of cast to afford the joining seams.

Note. Soak casts in water 5 minutes before starting to put in plastic wood.

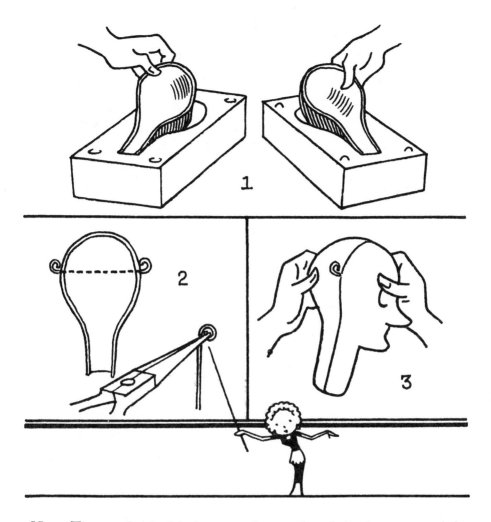

Note. Tie two finished halves together, and soak in water over night.

1. Gently pull head out, and allow to dry.

2. Bore small hole just above where ear would be and place wire through, making loops of ends of wire with sharp nosed pliers.

3. Finished head ready for drying and hardening.

Note. Wire may be placed in head before putting parts together. Be sure the cast is perfectly dry before boring hole.

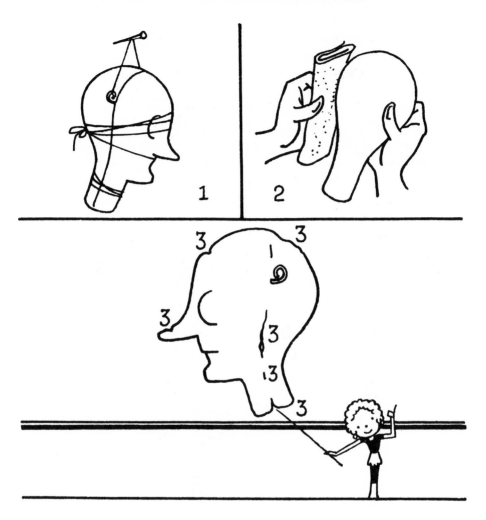

1. Tie string in loops of wire and hang up on safe nail somewhere.

2. When completely dry and hard, sandpaper surface until smooth, first with very rough sandpaper, finishing with very fine, being careful not to destroy character.

3. If small imperfections show up, more plastic wood can be added to correct same, and sandpaper again.

Note. If head is put in hot water at once while mending, plastic wood will not shrink.

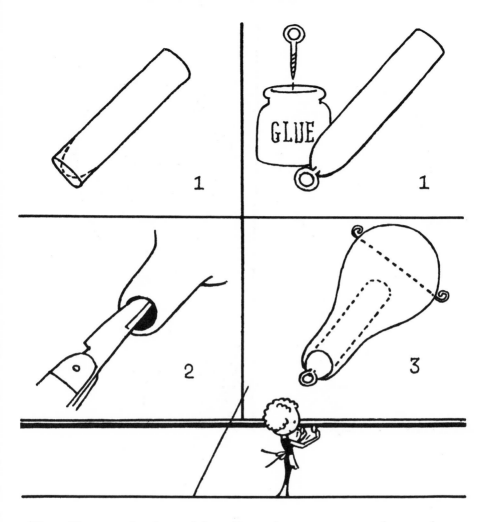

Note. Have ready piece of doweling, glue, screw eye and a wood rasp.

1. Shape one end of dowel with pen knife and wood rasp to make a half cone and put screw eye in center after dipping the point in glue to insure against pulling out.

Note. Screw eyes will not hold in plastic wood unless glue is used.

2. Shape inside of neck to fit wood core with knife and sandpaper.

3. Smear core with glue, push up into head and lay aside to dry.

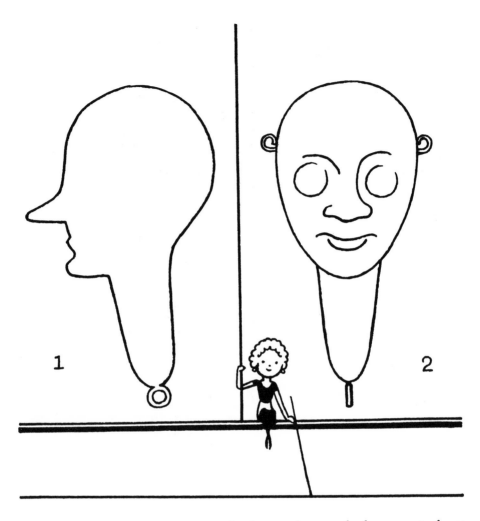

1. When glue is dry, put more plastic wood around edge so as to form half cone which will fit into shoulders later.

2. Head is now completed ready for finishing.

Note. Gesso treatment. See page 37 for details. Also pages 38-39 for paint and finish details.

Note. Wire may be used for neck by making loops and filling in necks with plastic wood, if screw eyes are not available.

Note. Paper-mache is a much less expensive and better method of moulding heads. Have ready white paper napkins, pieces of strong wrapping paper, bowl of water, and wall paper paste, saucer and your cast.

1. Mix enough wall paper paste in saucer with water to form a paste of the consistency of thick cream.

2. Tear—do not cut—paper napkins in very small pieces.

3. Smear paste on pieces of paper with fingers.

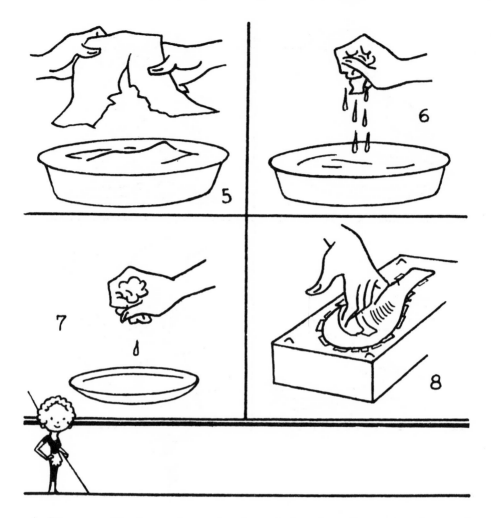

4. Place small pieces about the size of thumb nail overlapping and press down smooth until one layer overall of inside of the cast.

5. Tear up wrapping paper in small pieces and place in water.

6. When well soaked, squeeze out surplus water.

7. Cover this with paste, working it well into the paper.

8. Place in mould same as first layer, and use at least six layers of this.

Note. Alternate layers of different colored paper, help to check on number of layers.

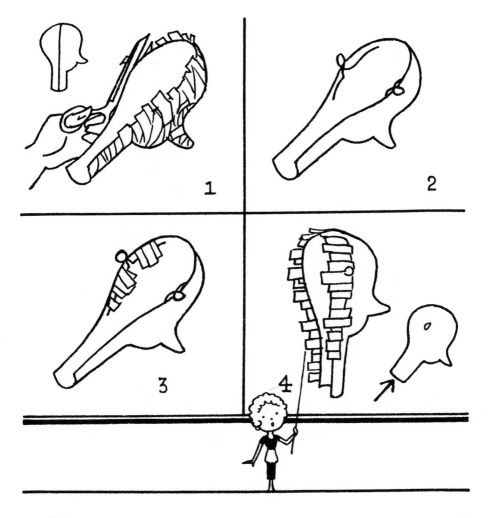

1. When halves are dry and hard, trim the edges so that they fit together perfectly.

2. Place wire inside before putting together the two pieces.

3. Anchor to insides with paper-mache. Place small pieces of paper-mache to front half of head, always overlapping edges.

4. Press back and front part of head together and smooth down pieces of paper-mache so that both halves stick together. Keep adding more paper-mache until all is strong and smooth. Also add some paper-mache to inside of head as far as you can reach. Allow to dry.

Note. Ears may be modeled on after head is dry, but usually not necessary, as hair, etc. cover them.

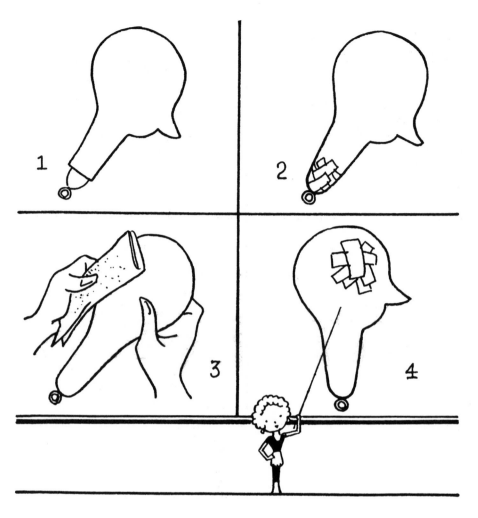

1. When perfectly dry and hard, put core of wood as described in plastic wood neck, using piece of dowel, screw eye, glue, etc.

2. Finish off head by placing paper-mache over edge of neck down to screw eyes to make a smooth cone shape.

3. Use very fine sandpaper to smooth entire head.

4. If any defects are noticed they can be fixed up with more paper-mache and building up to sufficient hardness and thickness.

Note. Hardness and thickness may be determined by holding up to light.

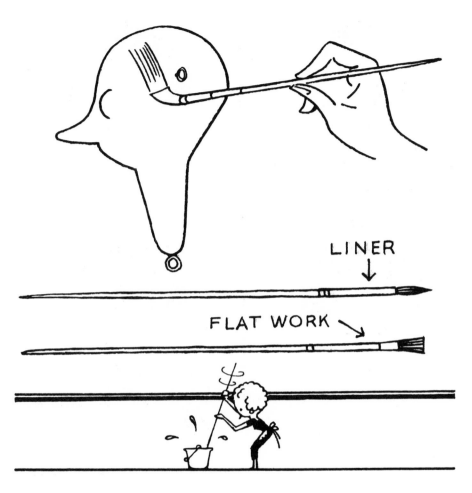

LINER

FLAT WORK

After head is finished and ready, it must be given a preliminary coat of paint of water color or oil as a foundation complexion. Shade used will be determined by character. Oil colors are best, but it is necessary to dull the finished head with very fine sandpapering. Water colors or tempera may also be used.

Note. Procure white, black, scarlet vermilion, new blue, chrome yellow, light veredian green, burnt sienna, and brushes. Brushes necessary—small liner, larger brush for flat surface, and a stippling brush.

1. White, some yellow.

2. Same as Chinese—add very little burnt sienna to lean toward tan.

3. Burnt sienna—add black or white to darken or lighten.

4. Burnt sienna with white and very little red to lean toward pink.

Note. Turpentine and dryer. Have ready **a** small amount of each.

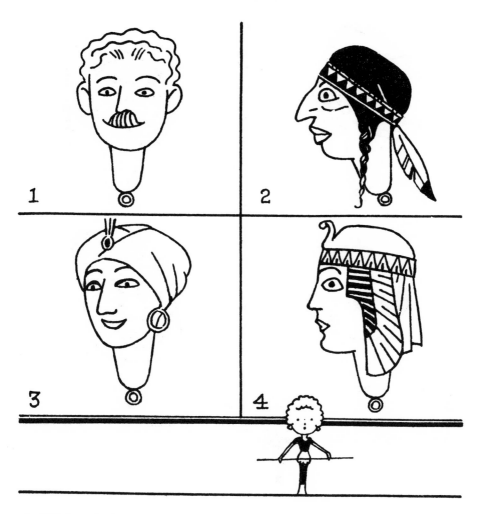

1. White, slight yellow and enough red to bring out flesh color.

2. White with little red and enough burnt sienna to give a copper color.

3. Burnt sienna with a touch of pink and yellow.

4. Same as Indian with a little black.

1. Same as Caucasian flesh tint with little burnt sienna added.

2. Same as Italian with a deeper tan effect.

3. Same as Caucasian only a straight pink, no yellow.

4. All white.

Note. On clown and ghastly witches, etc. a phosphorescent effect helps.

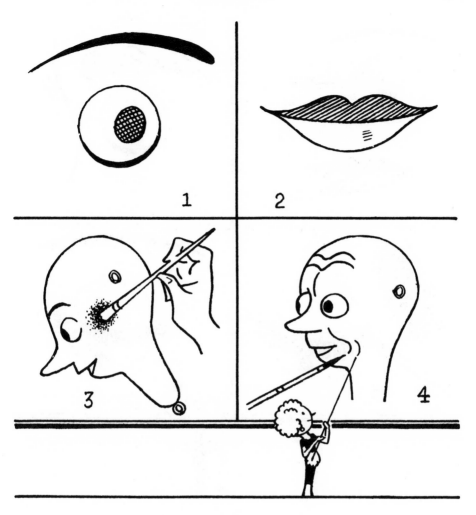

1. Eyes, eye-balls should be underlined.

2. Lips, lip modeling must be clearly defined with paints.

3. Stipple to spread color gradually and to blend.

4. Wrinkles, emphasize with thin lines.

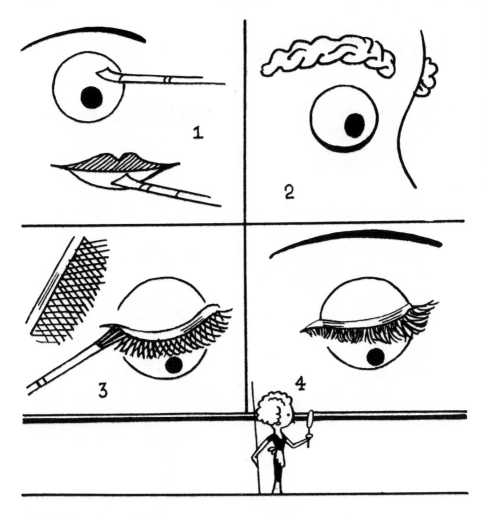

1. Shellac eyes and lips to liven up expression of face.

2. Eyelashes lined out of wool or silk glued on to lids.

3. Eyelashes made of bias cut buckram and glued on and then painted.

4. Fur strips glued on to lids.

Note. Eyelash effect can be had with carefully painted lines.

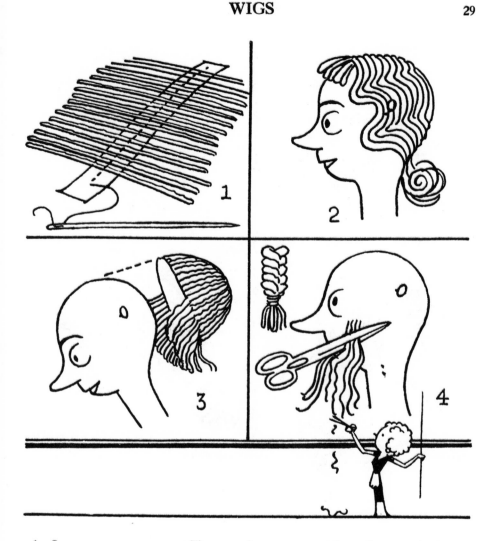

1. Sew yarn on to tape. Tape to be as near color of yarn chosen as possible. Glue to head.

2. Yarn glued directly to head and dressed later, such as curls, braids, buns, etc.

3. Yarn sewed first on a fitted cap and cap glued or tacked to head.

4. Shredded rope, yarn or crepe hair glued on and trimmed for beard.

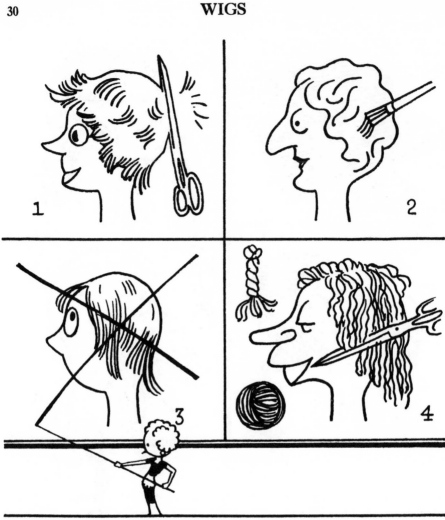

1. Fur may be cut to shape and glued on head.

2. Hair may be painted directly on to head, especially when it has been indicated in the original model.

3. Human hair wigs may be used but not recommended.

4. Frayed rope, silk floss or crepe hair is a good substitute for human hair effect.

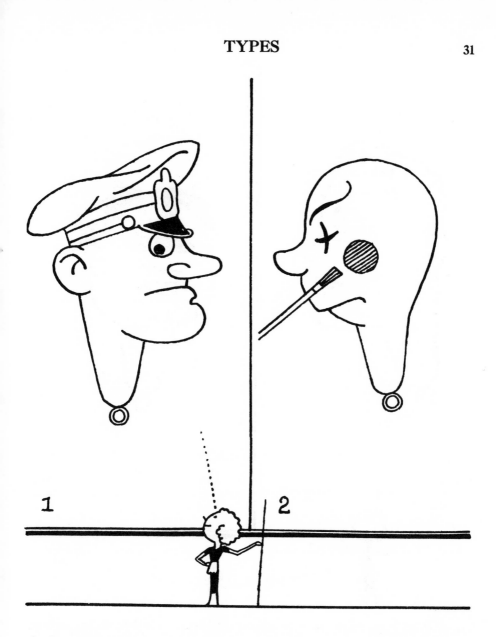

1. Should be forceful—emphasize strong jaw—nose small and funny, weather-beaten—eye that seems to be taking everything in.

2. Clown must be jovial—roundness and fullness helps—spots, painted on face. bring a supercilious expression a real clown has.

1. A *hero* type must be everything desirable, good-looking, strong, healthy—his features must be rather regular, inclined to the athletic sort.

2. Character to play the part of a *bully* must be made to look selfish, a wide head for combativeness, a turned-down mouth, heavy jowls, eyes rather close.

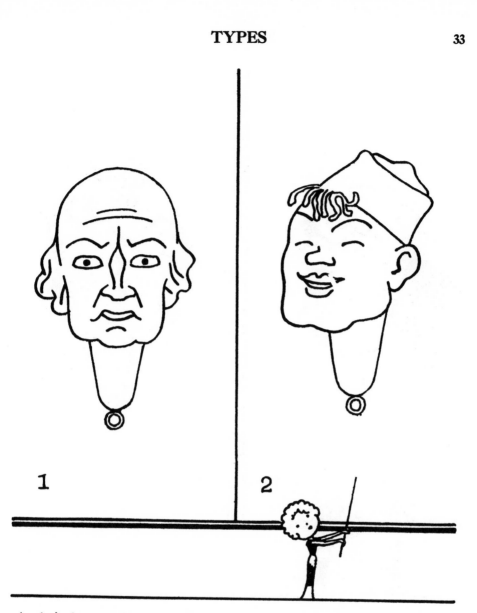

1. A *judge, professor* or such, to have high, intellectual forehead—
to seem commanding—and to have an air of refinement.

2. The *sailor* is usually expected to appear carefree—ruddy complexion—usually smiling, squint eyes, and every touch that portrays an
out-of-doors man.

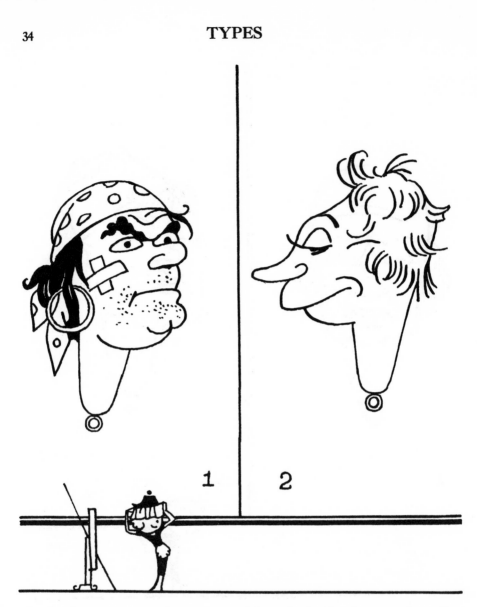

1. A *pirate* may vary in type—combines the bully, the cop, the sailor,

   etc., except that he must be above all, hard-boiled—with a sabre scar

   and a black eye.

2. The *simpleton* is a sort of clown plus a foolish and weak expression

   —little chin—long nose—eyes that cast down-ward.

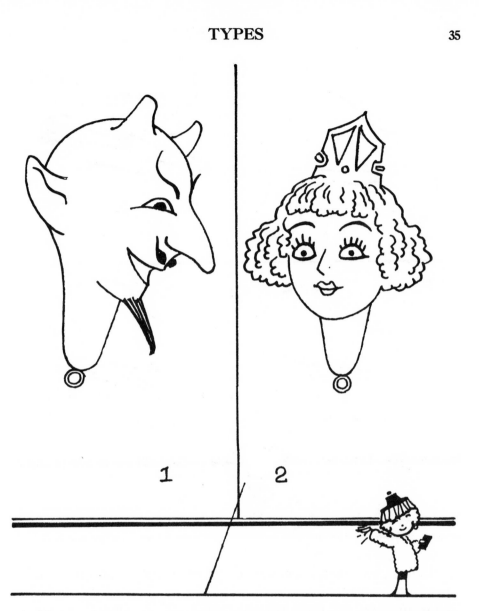

1. The *devil* must be sleek—his grin must naturally be devilish—his ears and nose must bring out his character without depending upon his horns. Red and silver mica cloth may be pasted on eyes to give shiny effects.

2. A *queen, fairy, princess type,* to bring out beauty. No exaggerations, except in color. Compared with all other marionette types these must be dainty.

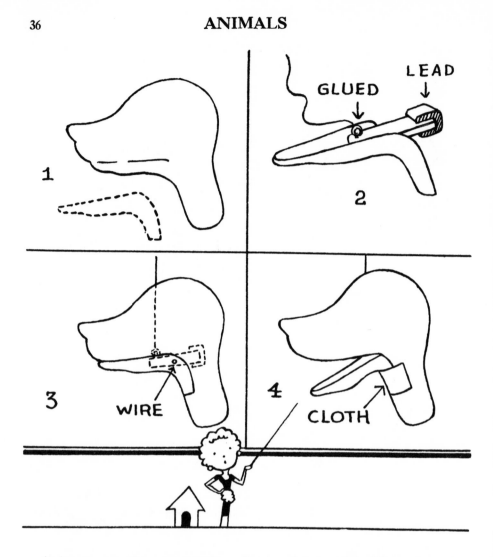

Animals are often needed for plays and it is advisable as in some cases with human types to use a movable jaw. These heads must be hollow to allow for inside construction.

1. When your animal head is finished, and before it is painted, cut away the lower jaw carefully.

2. Add to this jaw a piece of wood, which must be weighted with sheet lead or lead weights at the back part. Cut away a small part of the neck construction just back of the jaw to allow for slight movement.

3. Replace the jaw and hinge it with a straight piece of wire through the sides of the head and through the wood. Fasten on to the other side just at the junction of the jaw.

4. The lead weighting will keep the mouth closed, but a string attached to the lead weight passed up through a hole in the top of the head will, when pulled straight up, allow the jaw to open. When the string is slack the mouth closes.

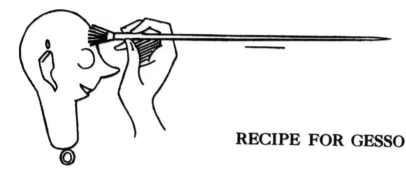

RECIPE FOR GESSO

If after completing your marionette a very smooth surface is desired, an excellent way to produce this is to give it a gesso finish especially for the face and hands and exposed parts of the body.

Gesso is a finish composed of rabbit's skin glue and whiting. Soak 1 sheet of glue in a quart of water overnight, or about six or eight hours. Then heat and bring slowly to a boiling point. With a soft brush give object two or three coats of this glue mixture. Let it dry thoroughly. Then add a little of the whiting, keeping mixture very thin. Next, brush object with this. Then add a little more whiting.

Repeat this process a few times until desired surface is obtained. If a shiny surface is desired, finish with a coat of glue without whiting.

 Procure a wooden palette or a piece of glass or an old flat dish to use as a mixing base. Squeeze a small amount of colors chosen onto this surface. Add a small amount of turpentine and dryer and begin to mix and blend colors to arrive at the proper shades needed, using medium size paint brush.

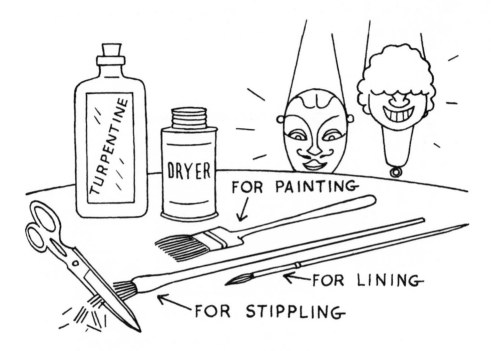

Use this same brush to put on first color coats.

Use smaller brush for shadows and lining. A stipple-brush may be made by cutting a larger stiff bristle brush straight across evenly, although such a brush may be bought at art stores. This brush is used dry and clean to blend colors already applied, as on cheeks and shadows. Be sure to clean all brushes after each painting operation, using turpentine to loosen paint, and then washing the brushes with soap and water, drying carefully and smoothing to points.

Procure a bag of wall-paper, or Fox, paste at any hardware store.

Use only a small amount at a time, mixing with cold water to a paste of the consistency of mayonnaise. This paste costs little and will give better results if not allowed to become stale.

If a small quantity of ordinary glue is mixed with the paste, one teaspoonful of glue to a teacup of paste, the resulting surface will be harder and stronger. Beat with a fork or spoon until very smooth. This may be applied with a brush or with the fingers.

DULL FINISH FOR HEADS THAT HAVE BEEN PAINTED WITH OIL-COLORS

Oil colors being the best medium for painting marionette or puppet heads, sometimes appear too shiny when finished. This finish seems to reflect the light too much and it is best to obtain a duller effect.

Use either the finest grained sandpaper obtainable or better still— soft steel wool. Rub gently over the surface of the face after all painting is finished and completely dry and hard.

The eyes and lips may then be shellaced again. This last process will cause lights to be reflected, and will give a very enlivening effect every time the marionette moves the slightest bit.

This also applies to the finish of the hands and feet. Finger-nails and toe-nails may also be shellaced to give a livelier effect.

A puppet is ideal to use as an announcer for a marionette show either pushed through a slit in the curtain or through a small opening in the side. With a few jolly jokes and remarks he can outline the story or plot, picture the characters, and amuse the audience.

A puppet is a figure using the covered hand of the manipulator to bring it to life. You know them as the characters in the familiar Punch and Judy shows. The heads of these amusing little people are made along the same lines of construction as the marionette heads, with a slightly different method of finishing.

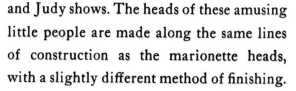

After the modeling, moulding and build-up of the head as described in the first part of this book is completed, you may come to the decision of using it for a hand puppet instead of a marionette.

If you are clever at carving you may want to make a head of balsa-wood. This is a light soft wood, easy to cut with a good pen-knife. A block of this kind of wood 3″ x 3″ x 5″ would make a head of proper size. Then proceed to hollow out the neck piece so as to allow plenty of room for the first finger to fit into it snugly.

Instead of the solid wood-neck construction of the marionette heads, the inside of the head and neck are left hollow with a smooth finish at the neck line.

These heads may be varied, as to character, the same as the marionette heads; animals or clowns, being ideal for puppets.

Animals should have paws, claws or hoofs according to the animal wanted. These may be made of stuffed cloth or of carved wood, and inserted in edge of sleeve instead of the hands of human characters.

Legs may be sewed on the outside of the under-sleeve and are generally stuffed with cotton, with a stitching at the knee joint. A long under-sleeve of dark material is made for the purpose of masking the movements of hand and arm.

The first finger of the hand is for the head and the thumb and forefinger for the arms. When you crook your first finger the

puppet nods and bows. When you waggle your thumb or forefinger, the arms will wave about. The puppet can be made to hold various articles in its hands.

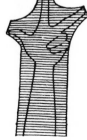

Making
Marionette Hands,
Feet, Legs, Arms
and Bodies

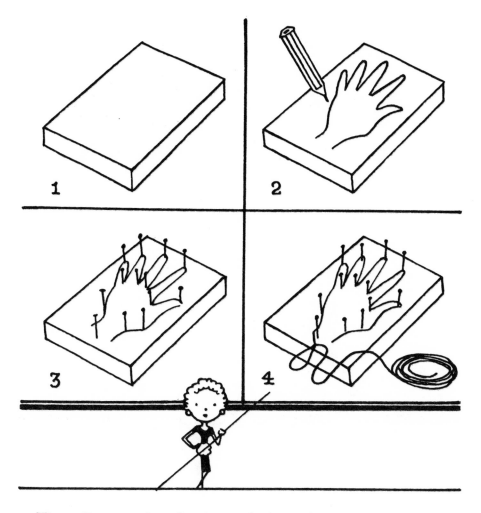

These diagrams describe the method of using wire, wax and tape.

1. Cut a block of wood about 3 x 4 inches for an armature.

2. Outline in pencil a drawing of a hand, using your own hand as a guide.

3. Drive ½ inch pin nails around the drawing as the dots indicate.

4. Use #16 wire (copper is best) and place around the nails, weaving and fastening with pliers to form a foundation (or bones) of a hand.

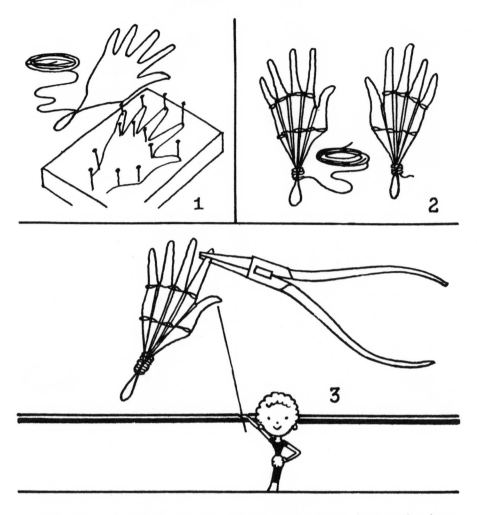

1. Slip carefully off of the nails, being careful not to destroy the shape.

2. Make another one. Turn it over and you have both a right and a left hand.

3. Shape and tighten with pliers, making the finger ends narrower than the base of the fingers. If larger or smaller hands are wanted make a larger or a smaller armature.

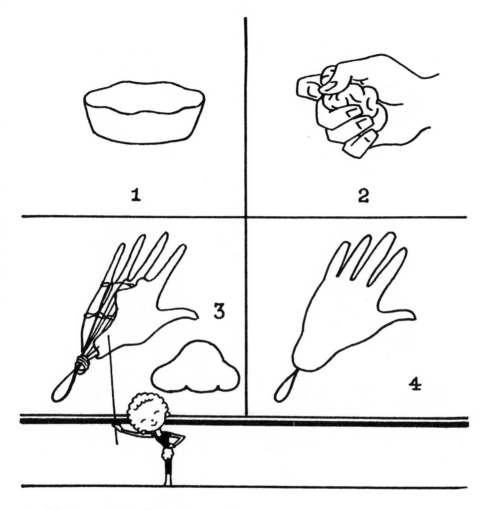

1. Have ready a cake of bees-wax.

2. Cut off a small piece. By kneading it with the fingers, the warmth of the hand will soften the wax.

3. Begin to place small pieces of the wax over the wire, covering and shaping fingers, thumb, palm, wrist, etc. This may be called "flesh or muscles."

4. Leave wire loop free at the wrist without covering with wax. Model your hand to suit the character you have chosen.

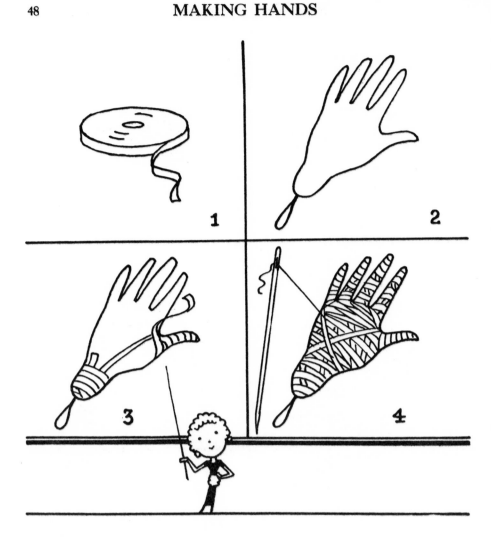

1. Have ready a roll of silk binding tape.

2. The wax covered hand ready for covering.

3. Begin to wrap the hand carefully in a diagonal direction, covering all parts of the hand and all parts of the fingers.

4. With a needle and thread catch the loose parts and edges, and make all firm, so the wax cannot escape through the edges of the tape, when the fingers are bent.

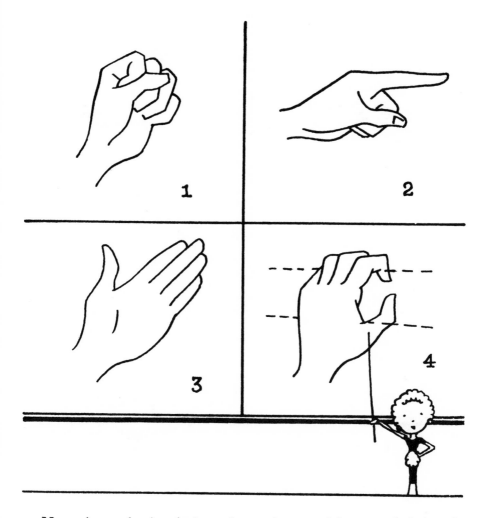

1

2

3

4

Now shape the hands into the various positions needed for the character you wish to create, such as,

1. Fist.

2. Pointing.

3. Open.

4. To hold various articles.

Be sure the finished thumb is shaped as in the illustration, to give a more lifelike appearance, and to avoid looking like "chicken feet."

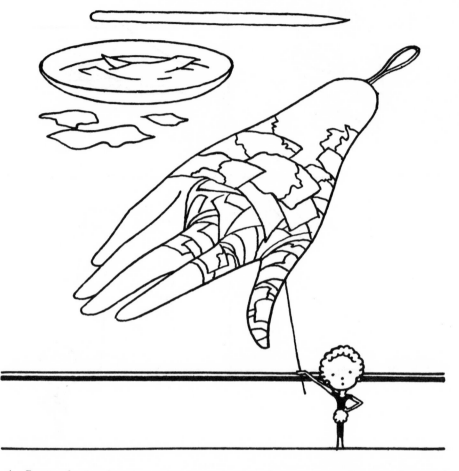

1. Instead of using tape to wrap the hand, paper-mache may be used to cover the bees-wax after the hand has been shaped in the correct position. The recipe for paper-mache will be found on page 39.

Use very small torn pieces of thin paper in making this covering and use the method of paper-mache before mentioned, being careful to have all surfaces very smooth.

A small orange stick will help in shaping and smoothing and defining wrinkles, veins, knuckles and nails. Allow to dry before painting.

The hand and forearm may be made in one piece if wrist action is not needed.

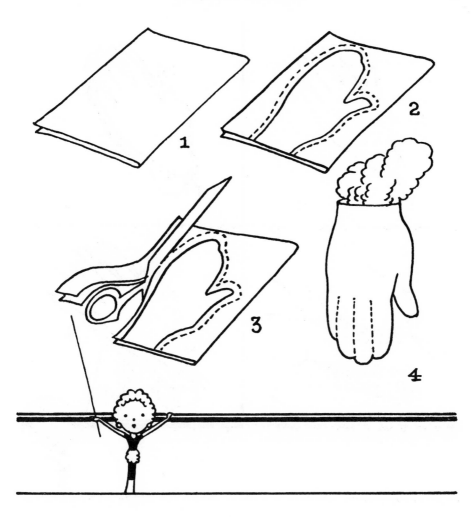

1. A folded piece of strong muslin.

2. With a lead pencil draw the pattern for the hand.

3. Cut two, being careful to allow ¼ inch for sewing seams. Sew around fingers ¼ inch from the edge. Then turn so that the seams are on the inside.

4. Stuff tightly with cotton, inserting a small piece of lead or a few lead shot for weighting. Be sure to always make right and left hands. Both cloth and chamois hands may be painted with oil or water-color to match the face. These hands may be sewed directly onto the cloth arms, or glued and tacked onto the wooden ones.

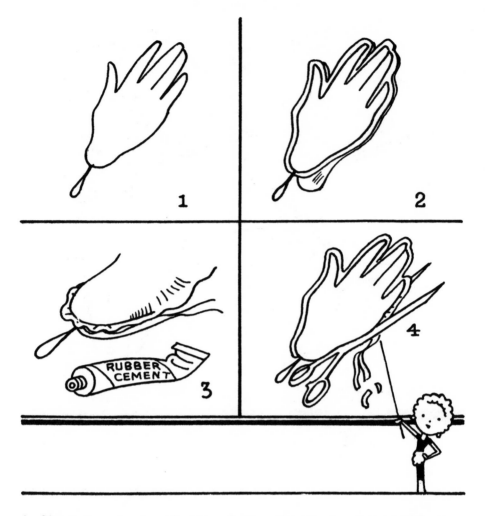

1. Shape the wire foundation as before described and model the wax shape.

2. Cut right and left pieces of chamois in patterns a little larger than the shape of the hand desired.

3. Coat the hand with rubber cement generously. Then place the chamois on the front and the back of the hand.

4. Press into place, bringing the edges together. Cut around the edges of the fingers and the rest of the hand with a pair of scissors. This closes and usually sticks the edges together. If any imperfections or gaps appear a few stitches will repair the break.

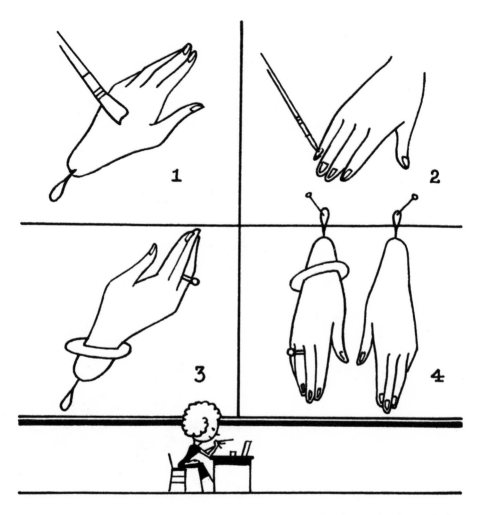

1. The hands may now be painted to match the complexion of the head. You may use oil, water-color, or tempera paints. The recipe for color values in detail will be found on pages 24-26.

2. The finger nails may be painted on.

3. Rings and other jewelry may be added, sewing or anchoring them securely.

4. Set aside, or hang on a convenient nail to dry in pairs.

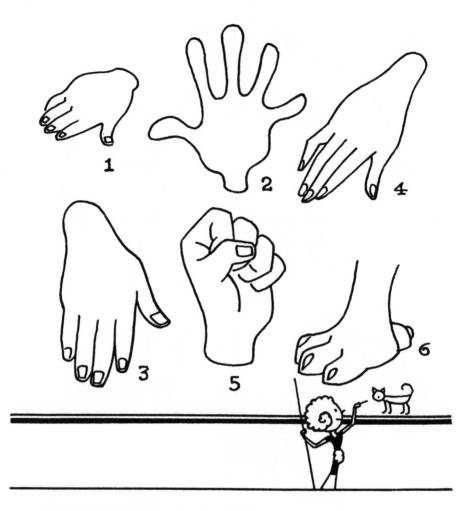

1. Baby hands—small, round, and fat.

2. Clown's hands—awkward and funny.

3. Man's hand—strong, virile, and usually larger.

4. Lady's hand—dainty.

5. A fist.

6. An animal's paw.

Sometimes a fist paired with an open hand will make a more interesting combination. All of these types may be made with any of the methods described in this book.

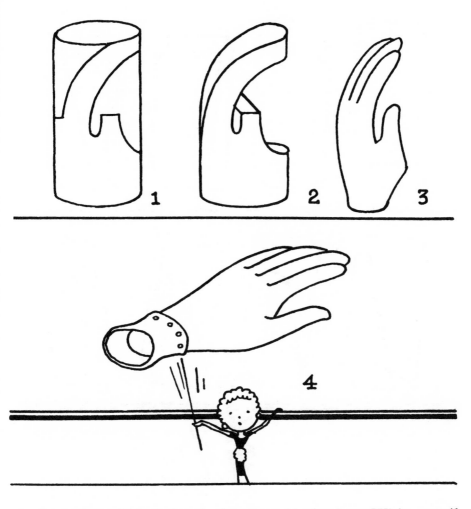

1. Cut a piece of 1 inch dowel-stick about 4 inches long. With a pencil draw lines as your picture indicates.

2. Place in a vise and with a saw and wood rasp, cut out and shape the indicated curves.

3. Round off with rasp and sandpaper for the shaping of the fingers and the wrist.

4. Finish nicely with sandpaper or pen knife (or better still, procure a good carving set). Be sure that the fingers are in proportion. Add indentations for finger nails, etc. Wrists are of chamois or cloth, fastened so as not to obstruct movement. Don't forget the left hand.

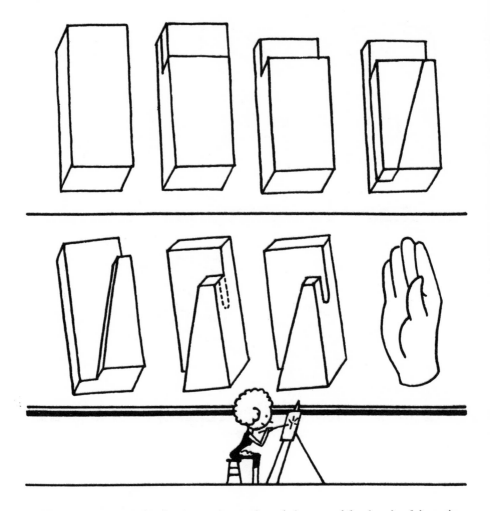

Here is one method of carving a hand from a block of white pine wood. With a pencil draw the lines as shown in the above drawings and make your cuts by sawing out the parts designated. Draw a new line before each sawing.

Finish with a wood rasp and sandpaper and now the hands are ready to paint.

With a little attention to detail you may create many types of hands. Never forget that the left hand must be the same size and general shape of the right one and be sure that they are mates.

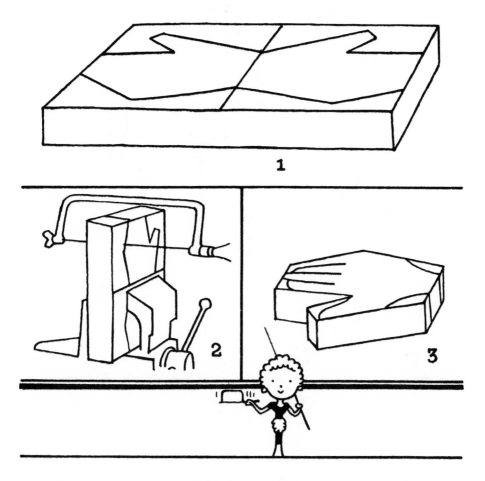

1. Hands may be carved directly from a white pine block of wood, 6 inches long, 2 inches wide, and ½ inch thick. With a pencil draw pattern of hand, right and left, so as to have both the same size. Draw the hands on tracing paper and reverse.

2. Place the hands in a vise and saw around the edge of the drawing.

3. Now whittle with a pen knife or chip away surplus wood with a chisel. Hand is then refined with sandpaper and painted to match complexion of the head.
   Carve in position of hand needed and indicate fingernails.

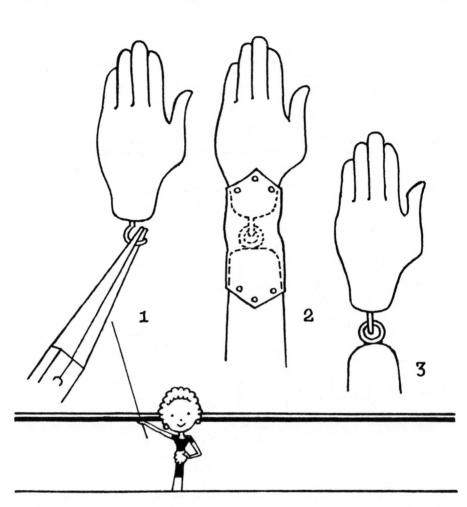

These diagrams describe the method of joining wooden hands onto the lower wooden arms.

Place a screw-eye in the center of the wrist and open the ring with a pair of pliers.

Place a screw-eye in the center of the lower wooden arms and join the rings. Close the rings.

Take a small piece of chamois and cover the screw-eye joint, tacking it on after a small smearing of glue is placed to reinforce same.

Allow for just enough movement such as a wrist action should have.

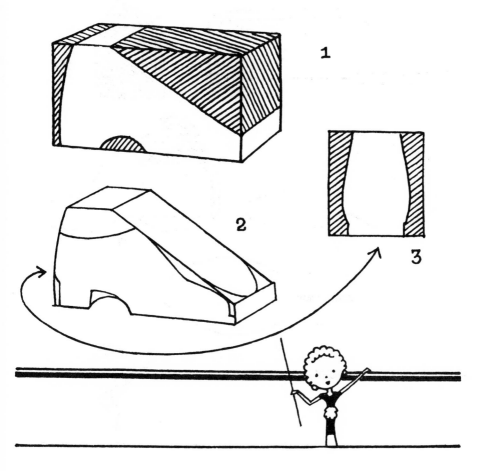

Wooden feet made of a block of white pine will hold their shape well; however if bass-wood can be obtained you will find that it is exceptionally easy to work with. This may be obtained in mill-end pieces from the lumber yards.

1. Shows the block of wood marked for the first cutting. Always outline with a pencil the next cutting line.

2. The first cutting ready for carving and shaping.

3. Back view of the shoe outlined for cutting the heel.

Always remember that the size of the foot should be exaggerated in proportion to the rest of the body.

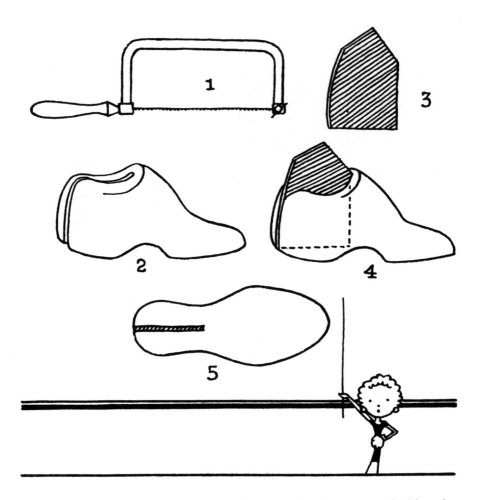

1. Have ready a piece of trunk fibre, and a sharp pen knife, glue, sandpaper, and a saw.

2. Cut a slot in the back part of the foot.

3. Cut a small piece of trunk fibre to fit in slot.

4. Place a piece of trunk fibre well covered with glue into the slot, allowing the exposed part to extend up above the shoe or the foot. This may be done in both the carved wood foot or the paper-mache and wax covered foot.

5. When dry, fill up all cracks with paper-mache or plastic wood. Paint and put aside to dry.

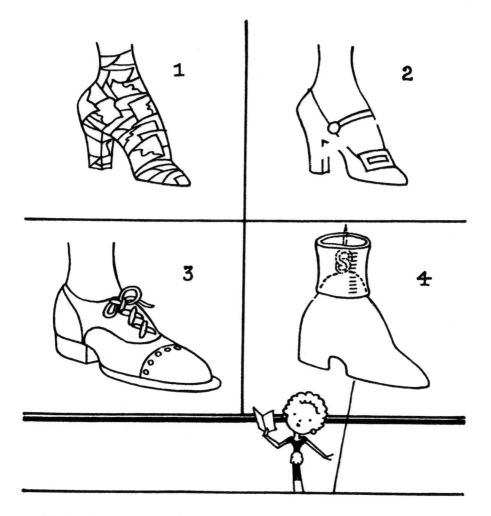

Make the paper-mache mixture. Obtain paper towelling. Tear it into very small pieces, and smear on the paste mixture. Tearing the paper towelling into very small pieces instead of cutting. It will give you an uneven edge. Always overlap these edges.

1. Cover the foot, using about two layers of the paper-mache.

2. With a modelling tool define sole of the shoe, buckles, straps, edges, or decorations.

3. Note the difference between a man's shoe and a woman's shoe.

4. This shows how a chamois covering may be used with the screw-eye joining. A stocking covering the entire foot and ankle may be used here and drawn up over the knee joint.

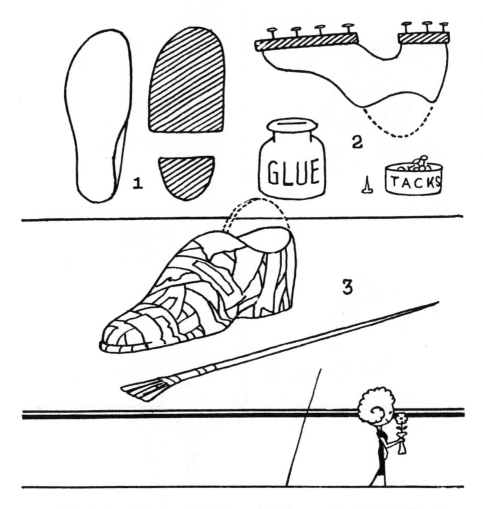

To make wooden feet heavy enough for manipulation, they must be weighted with lead. For this, use sheet lead or lead wool which may be shaped as desired by hammering.

1. Cut a piece of sheet lead 1/16 of an inch thick, just to fit the sole and the heel of the shoe.

2. Fit, cut, and pound to shape, then tack on to the bottom of the shoe, having first smeared the sole with glue. Do the same thing with the heel.

3. The shoe or foot is now ready to paint, but if you wish a nice smooth surface you may paper-mache all over the entire surface first.

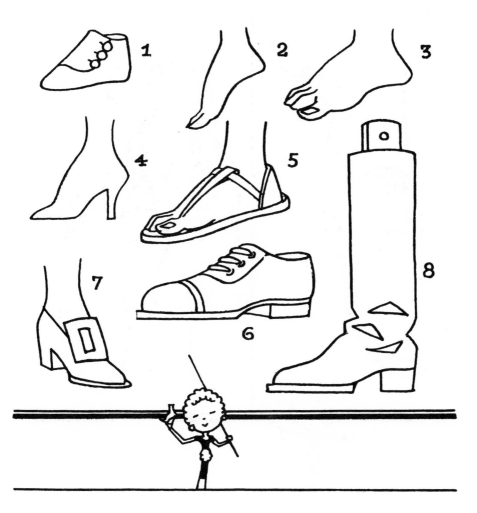

1. A baby's shoe.

2. A dancer's bare foot.

3. A bare foot—man.

4. A lady's slipper—high heels.

5. A Grecian sandal. This is easy to carve at time of making foot, or may be made of leather or cloth.

6. Man's heavy shoe.

7. Shoe with buckle. The buckle is either carved on the shoe or added to a leather slipper afterward.

8. A boot. The wrinkles are made with a rasp. This may be a boot and a lower leg carved in one with the joint such as you wish to use.

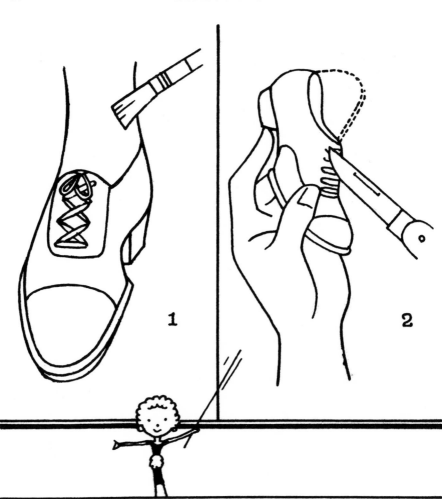

1

2

Now you are ready to paint your feet.

1. Paint the shoes with oil or water-color, choosing a color to fit your marionette character, or to harmonize with the costume.

2. All edges or imperfections may be smoothed with a pen knife and sand paper.

If stocking is to be shown (as with low shoes) be sure to paint stocking of a different color.

Buttons, ties or buckles may be painted on.

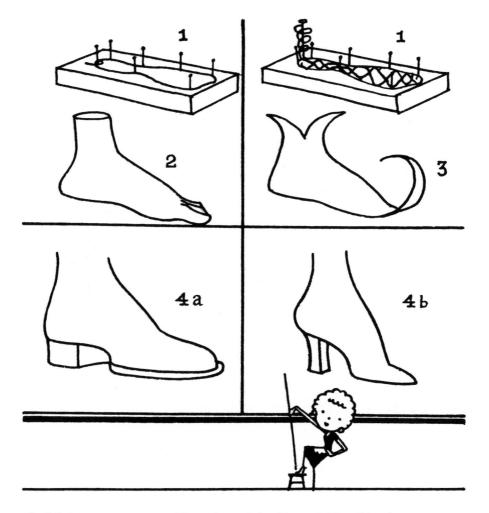

1. Make an armature. Use wire with pliers. Lift off in the same procedure as for the hands. Be sure to make right and left feet.

2. Modelled bare foot with bees-wax.

3. Modelled shoe, with bees-wax.

4. Shoes should have heels. (a) man's. (b) woman's. Bees-wax feet do not need weighting, as the bees-wax is heavy enough.

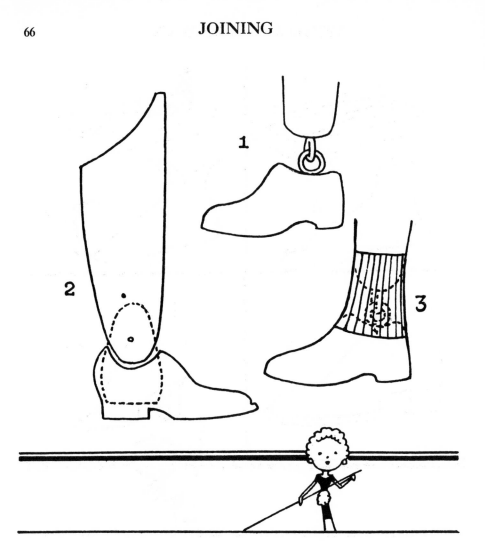

1. Screw-eye joining is an easy way to join the feet to the legs but you must either cover ankle with a stocking or use a chamois cuff. See fig. 3.

2. The trunk fibre joining is the best and strongest method.

3. Boot and leg joined with a screw-eye and covered with a cloth or chamois covering.

   Tin joints may be used, but they make too much noise.

   The legs should be carved so as to develop the real shape of the leg, especially where short trousers or skirts are used in the costume, or wherever the lower leg is exposed.

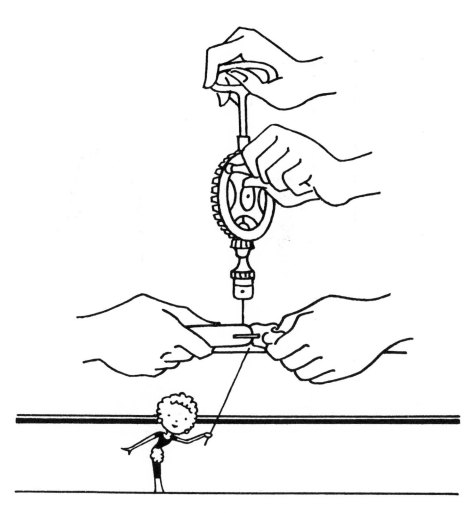

This diagram shows the best method of joining the feet to the legs.

You may need a helping hand here, so as to keep the job steady and to make for careful drilling.

Hold firmly in both hands, the leg and foot, with the fibre placed in the slot. Use the smallest drill.

Drill the hole through both pieces at one time, leaving just enough space for good movement.

Use small brads or wire to join the two parts together, bending back the surplus ends to fasten.

If the joint does not move easily and freely, take apart and sandpaper until this necessary detail is accomplished.

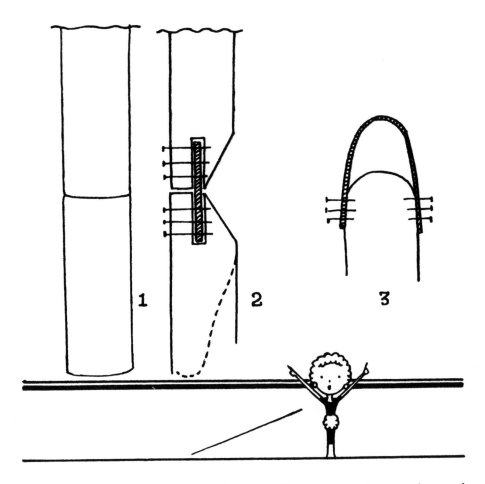

This diagram shows the use of small thin strong strips, or pieces of good leather cut in strips, for making a knee joint.

(Never use an old kid glove, as this stretches too easily.)

1. Cut a piece of dowel-stick the length of leg wanted. Saw it across, where you wish the knee joint to be.

2. Cut out the slots and shape the lower leg, not forgetting the slot at the ankle. Place the leather in the slots and use wire brads to fasten. Leave enough space between the joints for good movement.

3. This shows construction of this type of joint to be used for the shoulder.

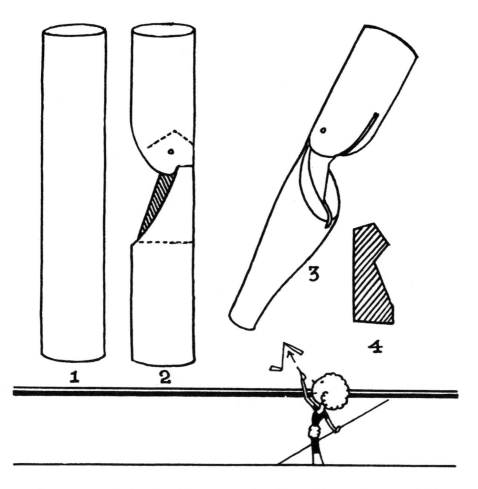

An easy method of making a wooden knee joint, using trunk fibre.

1. Cut a piece of 1¼ inch dowel about 6 inches long and cut it in two pieces. The upper leg piece should be 1/3 longer than the lower.

2. This diagram shows the fibre in place.

3. Here you may see the nicely rounded knee in the upper leg, also the opening in the back of the lower leg at the top. This makes for good action. Always remember to shape the lower leg.

4. The piece of trunk fibre cut in the shape necessary for joining the two parts of this joint. Be careful in the centering of the pin nail, and be generous with the glue in the slot you have cut. Excess glue may be wiped off before it dries.

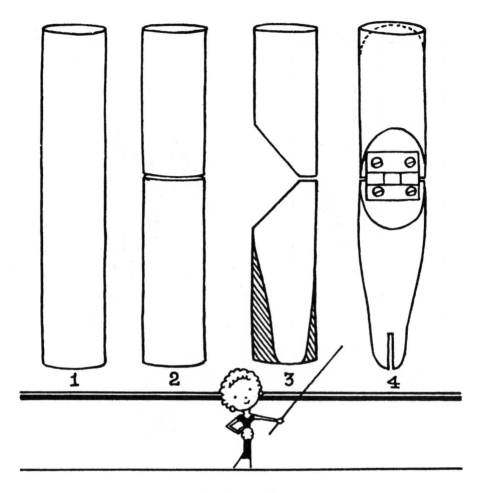

Method of knee joint using brass hinges.

1. Cut a piece of dowel-stick for the length of the leg needed.

2. Cut dowel-stick and make two pieces as described on previous pages.

3. With a coping saw cut out carefully the indicated parts and with a pen knife shape the lower leg. Do not forget the rounding of the ankle. Place in a vise to insure a steadiness in the cutting of the slot for the ankle. Sandpaper the slot for smooth action.

4. Procure a small pair of hinges and put them on carefully as the diagram shows. Round the top of the upper leg.

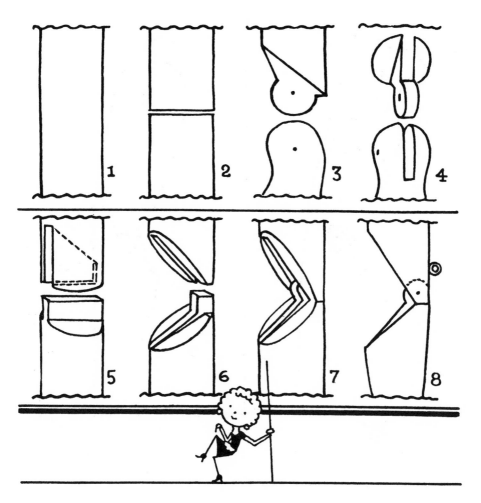

Another method for a wooden joint.

1. A piece of dowel-stick before cutting.
2. Cut apart as described in the other joints.
3. Shape with saw, wood rasp and sandpaper.
4. Round off and cut slots carefully.
5. The start of another type of wood joint.
6. The next step, cutting out the part in outline.
7. The joint rounded nicely, showing the joint placed.
8. The completed joint, showing a simple pin nail joining and placing of a screw-eye in the proper place, so as not to interfere with the movement.

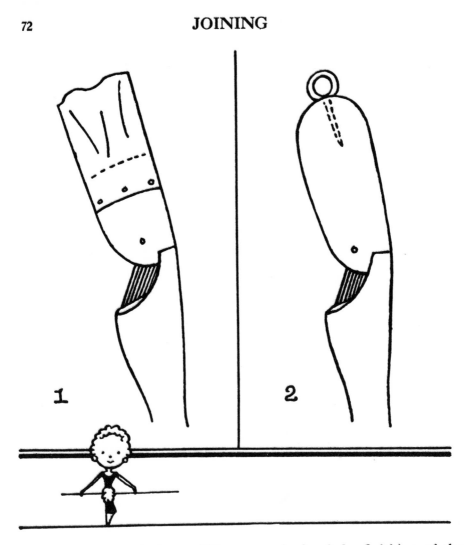

Here you will find two different methods of the finishing of the upper part of the leg, to make them ready for joining onto the torso.

1. Cut a piece of strong muslin. Glue, then tack this onto the upper part of the leg. Stuff part of this cloth with cotton. Allow one inch extra length of muslin to fold over for joining.

2. Round off the upper part of the leg and place a medium sized screw-eye into the center top. Dip your screw-eye into the glue. This will keep it from falling out.

A knee joint using the ball and socket and fibre joining.

1. The piece of dowel-stick before cutting.

2. A diagram showing how the lower leg is cut with the butterfly drill (6) to form a hollow socket. Also note how slots are now cut, ready for a piece of trunk fibre cut to shape.

3. Further cutting of the upper leg before shaping the ball part of the joint.

4. Complete joint rounded, with the trunk fibre placed.

5. Side view of the lower leg, showing socket gouged out with butterfly drill (6) and the slot for the fibre.

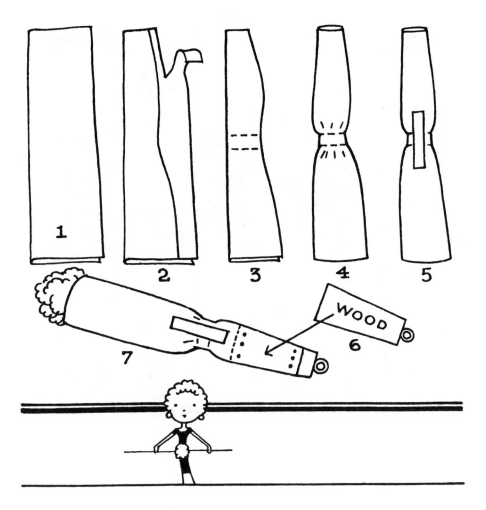

1. Here you have a folded piece of muslin. Cut two.

2. With a pencil draw a pattern line as the above diagram shows. Cut with a pair of scissors.

3. Sew two seams across the elbow joint.

4. Draw up the seams slightly.

5. Place a small piece of tape, tacking it above and below the elbow. This is a stop tape to prevent the arm from bending backward.

6. A piece of whittled wood to insert into the lower part of the sleeve. This allows you to put in a screw-eye at the wrist.

7. The upper part of the arm is very loosely stuffed to allow a free movement.

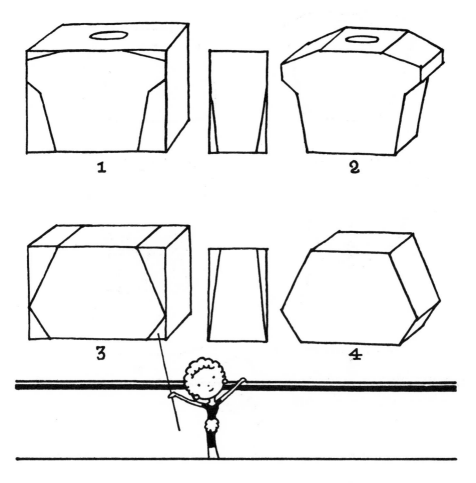

1. A block of wood with line penciled for cutting for the first step in making a shoulder piece. Use a 1 inch drill for the hole in the neck.

2. The shoulder piece cut and ready for shaping with the wood rasp and sandpaper.

3. A block of wood with lines penciled for cutting, for the first step in making a hip piece.

4. Hip piece cut and ready for shaping with the wood rasp and the sandpaper.

Place the block in a vise and cut around the lines with a saw. The use of white pine will be found very satisfactory and easier to handle than harder wood. Round all edges and shape nicely.

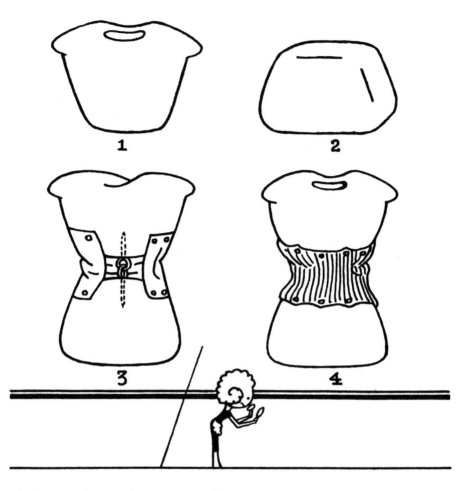

1. Finished shoulder piece ready for joining.

2. Finished hip piece ready for joining.

3. This diagram shows the method of using screw-eyes for joining the two parts. To lengthen this torso, place a piece of wire or chain between the screw-eyes.

4. This diagram shows the method of using a piece of stocking as a joining medium. Use glue to fasten before tacking it on. Marionettes have no stomach, and should be able to bend in every direction.

Keep trimming the parts for better action. The lengthening of a torso may be accomplished by a longer piece of stocking or a longer piece of wire.

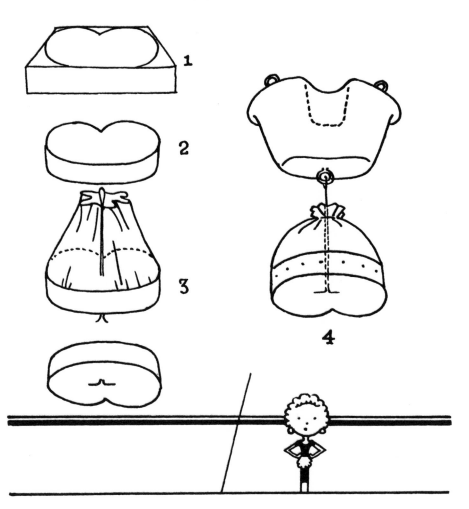

This is a different method of hip construction.

1. A block of wood penciled for cutting with the coping saw.

2. The hip piece cut out.

3. As this diagram shows, a strip of muslin is first glued and then tacked around the hip piece. Place a piece of wire through the center of the hip block. Double the wire back and down, and bend back the ends to fasten them, leaving a loop at the top.

4. Have the shoulder piece ready with a screw-eye inserted in the center. Fasten the wire from the hip piece to the screw-eye, by opening the screw-eye.

A piece of leather, or a chain, may be used instead of the wire; fastening back the ends underneath the hip piece.

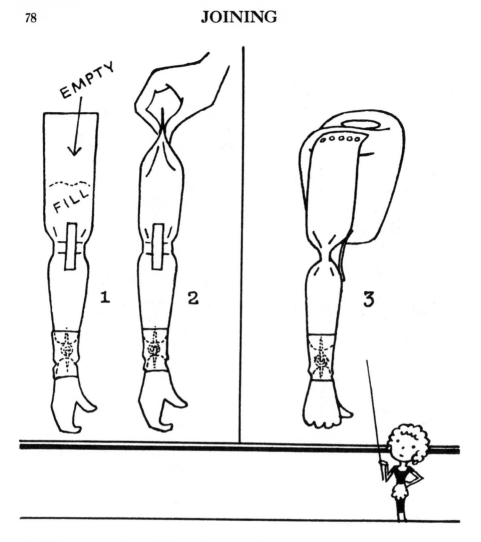

1. The arm ready to join to the shoulder.

2. This shows how the upper arm should be tacked on to the shoulder in an opposite direction to the seam at the elbow, to insure both the forward and the cross movement of the arms, when the arm strings are pulled.

   The upper arm should be very loosely stuffed.

3. The arms are to be fastened on with tacks and glue.

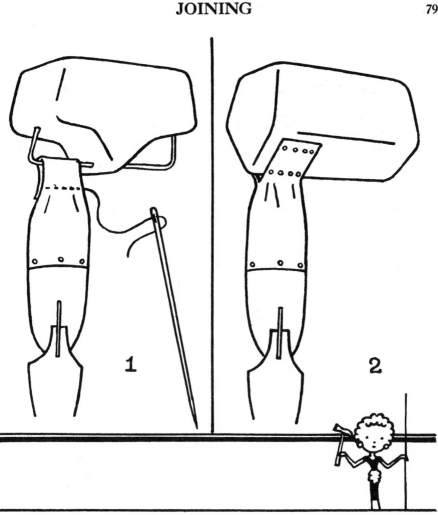

Now you are ready to join the legs to the torso.

1. Here you have a different type of a hip piece using a strong piece of wire. Before placing the wire, use a small drill to make the holes thru the wooden hip piece. To fasten the wire, bend over the ends. Now place the cloth top of the leg thru the wire, and stitch across the part indicated by the dotted line.

2. Here you split the cloth and tack it on both the front and back part of the hip piece. Leather may be used here instead of cloth.

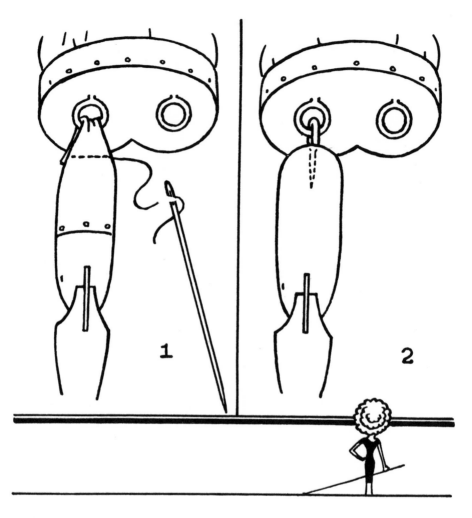

This diagram shows two other methods of joining the legs to the torso.

1. Here you may use the type of hip piece described in this book. Use very large screw-eyes, and be sure they are far enough apart for plenty of freedom of movement so that the legs may swing without interference.

2. With this method of joining, the upper leg must be rounded, and a medium sized screw-eye placed in the center of the upper leg.

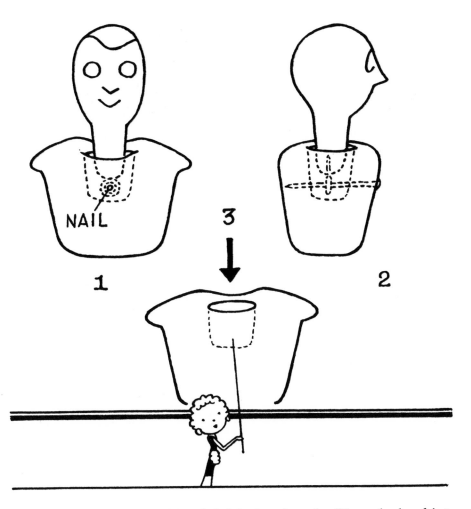

NAIL

1   3   2

1. Have your completed head finished and ready. Place the head into the space you have prepared in the upper part of the torso. When you find it moves freely in every direction, drive a long nail through the chest and through the screw-eye attached to the neck piece of the head. Be sure the nail is long enough to extend all the way thru the torso.

2. This diagram shows the side view of the above operation.

3. Here is shown the chest piece prepared for the joining. Use a one inch drill. Round with wood rasp and smooth with sandpaper.

Toy animals may be purchased and if their size is in scale they may be articulated for movement and stringing by cutting off the legs and the head, using the wire or chamois joining.

A wire may be thrust through the legs and the body so that the legs dangle loosely. Sew patches over the places cut out.

1. A toy dog, which you may purchase.

2. The dog and the parts cut away.

3. This shows the method of sewing the pieces of chamois after a part of the stuffing has been removed. The ears and tail are stitched on loosely.

4. This shows the neck with the stuffing removed, so that the neck is very loose.

A very easy method for small children to make a cloth stuffed marionette.

Joints are simply tied.

Feet and hands may be weighted for easier manipulation.

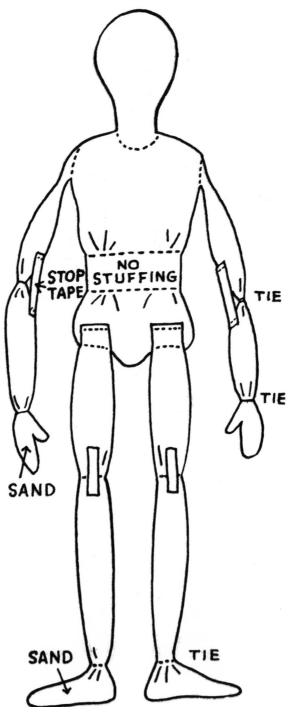

An easy rag doll type of marionette to make with cloth stuffed with cotton and the feet and hands weighted with sand or lead weights.

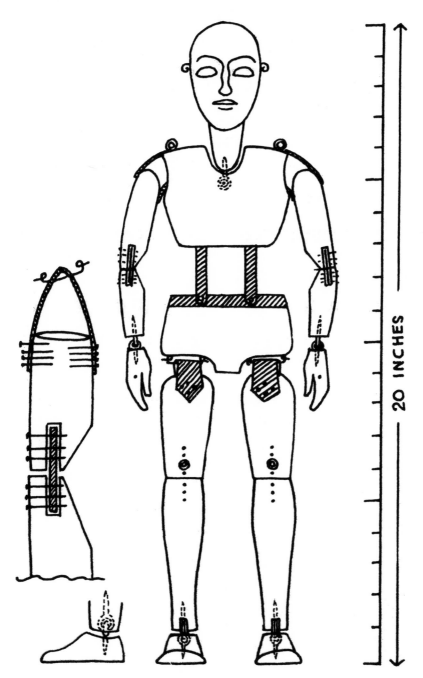

A scale and diagram skeleton of a marionette, ready for costuming and stringing.

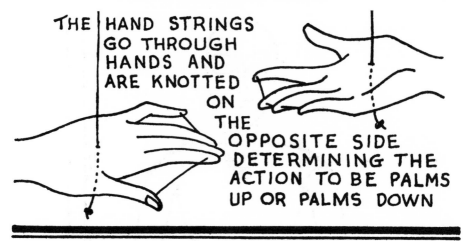

THE HAND STRINGS GO THROUGH HANDS AND ARE KNOTTED ON THE OPPOSITE SIDE DETERMINING THE ACTION TO BE PALMS UP OR PALMS DOWN

The hands—On wooden hands, screw-eyes may be used or a hole bored through the hand, the string passed through it and secured with a knot.

The legs—The screw-eyes are placed just above the knee, being careful not to interfere with the knee movement.

The head—The screw-eyes must be placed at each side of the head just above the ears. If you wish the head to droop, place them a little further back. If you wish the head to be very erect, place them a little further forward.

The shoulder—Place the screw-eyes on the outer edge of each shoulder.

The back—Place the screw-eye in the middle of the back as near the waistline as possible. By placing the screw-eye on each hip, you can make the side wiggle a hula dancer may need. To accomplish a forward kick, place the screw-eye in the toe. For a back kick place one in the heel.

The very smallest screw-eyes should be used.

These screw-eyes must be placed before starting to costume the marionette.

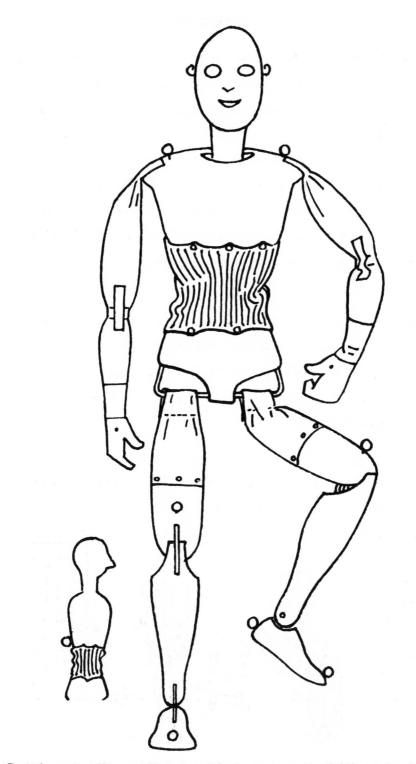

Complete wooden marionette, showing screw eyes for stringing.

The marionette on the opposite page is a copy of one belonging to the author. By giving attention to the details of careful modelling, carving and costuming, you can make replicas or caricatures of famous people. There is much educational benefit derived in accomplishing the many mechanical details in constructing the marionettes, even when their final characters have evolved and determined themselves at random. The real art and its thrill, however, is to be attained when the entire expression of the marionette is pre-determined and finally made to portray specifically a certain personage.

While even the crudest marionettes give a refreshing illusion of realism, the real living demention that attends them when the likeness of not only the face and type, but the little intimate actions and idio-syncracies are portrayed is a joy that makes it a blessing that there should be such an art.

Imagine the personification of one of your family or friends or a faithful little replica of your favorite movie star, coming into life to make fun of themselves and controlled by you.

A finished marionette costumed and strung ready for manipulation.

Stringing
and Manipulating
Marionettes

1 piece of lattice wood 10" x 1" x ¼".

1 piece of lattice wood 7" x 1" x ¼".

1 piece of lattice wood 9" x 1" x ¼".

1 piece of leather ¾" wide and 7" long.

3 small screw-eyes.

1 inch of ¼" doweling for the hanging of the foot-bar.
Glue—tacks.

The tools needed. A coping saw, ¼" drill, vise, file, pliers, hammer, brads, sandpaper and a light rope.

3 pieces of lattice wood 9" x ¼".

1 piece of lattice wood 7" x ¼".

String (See Page 98).

3 screw-eyes.

Glue.

The tools needed are the same as for the two-hand control.

Be sure to dove-tail the cut for joining of the cross pieces.

The slot in the end of the pieces must be small enough to hold the string firm before wrapping it around the notches.

The strap is for the purpose of hanging your finished marionette when it is strung ready for use.

The screw-eye underneath the control is for the running shoulder strings.

The two small screw-eyes on the front of the control are for the running hand strings.

All parts must be sandpapered smoothly for neatness and to prevent the catching of strings on any imperfections.

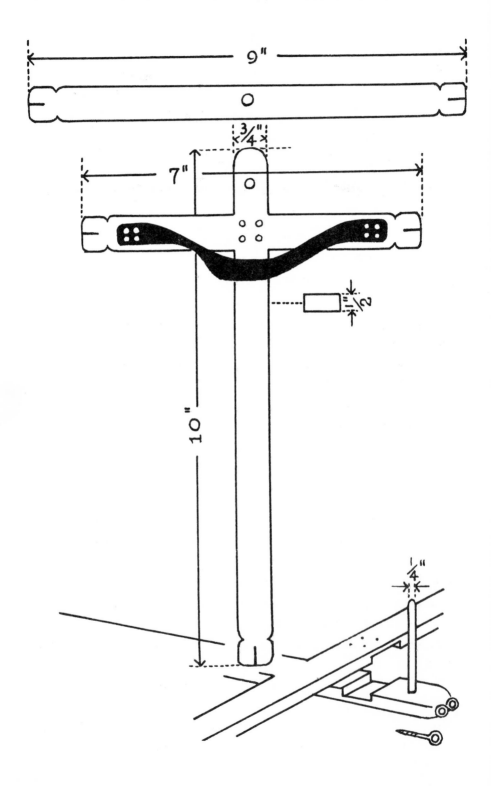

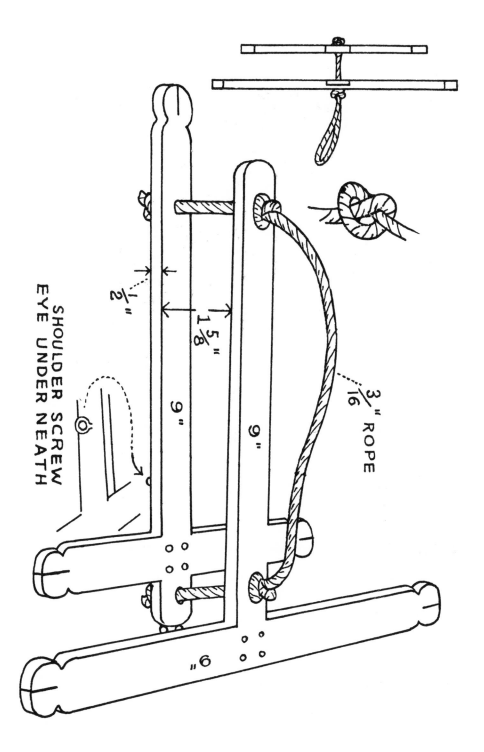

SHOULDER SCREW
EYE UNDER NEATH

$\frac{1}{2}$"

$1\frac{5}{8}$"

9"

9"

$\frac{3}{16}$" ROPE

9"

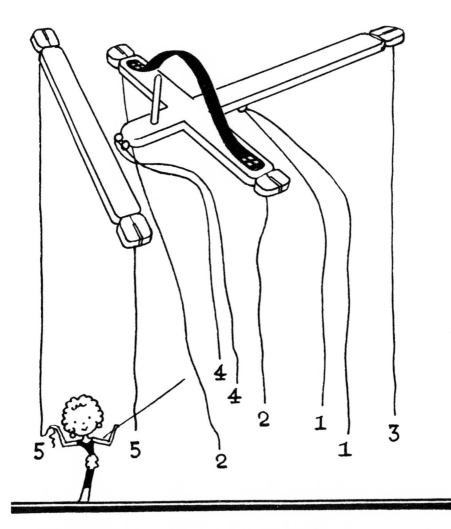

1. Shoulder string is a continuous running string.

2. Head strings.

3. Back string.

4. Hand strings are continuous running strings.

5. Foot strings.

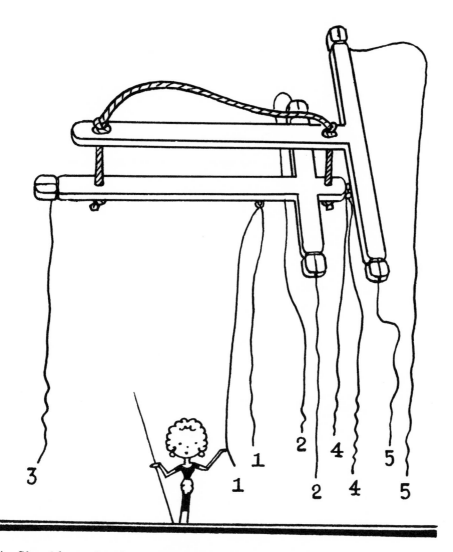

1. Shoulder string is a continuous running string.

2. Head strings.

3. Back string.

4. Hand strings are continuous running strings.

5. Foot strings.

STRINGING YOUR MARIONETTE

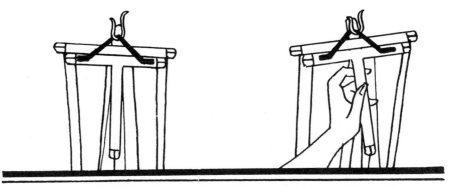

Now that your marionette is completed, your control finished and your marionette costumed, you are ready for stringing. String should be of a quality for strength. Ten pound test black silk fishline is the best for stringing purposes. It does not tangle so readily and resists wear and tear. However, if this is not available, a good stout linen thread may be used. Always use a square knot in this process.

Hang up your control by its leather strap on a convenient nail or hook, at the exact distance from the floor as you will hold it, when it is in use from your particular stage height.

String shoulder strings first.

This is to be a continuous running string, so cut a piece of string several inches longer than twice the distance from the control to the marionette's shoulder.

Tie one end with a square knot to the left shoulder. Carry the other end up to the control, pass it through the suspended screw-eye, marked "shoulder string," and back to the right shoulder, tying securely.

The weight is now suspended from the shoulder strings; these strings must be taut at all times, if they are allowed to become slack, the head movements will be stiff.

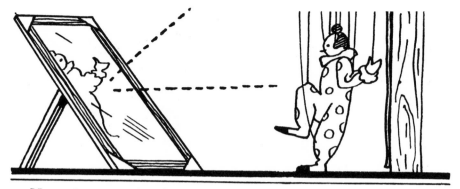

Now place your head strings.

Tie one string to the wire loop at the left side of the head. Measure the distance to your control, always allowing a few extra inches of string for possible lengthening later. Cut the string. Carry the other end up to the left side of the cross-bar marked left head string, pull it through the slot in the end of the wood, wrap the excess string around it, and fasten again into the slot.

Do the same thing with the other head string. Start with tying it to the wire loop near the right ear, and carrying up to the right of the cross-bar marked, "right head string."

Head strings must always be in front of the shoulder strings.

Next comes your back string.

Measure for length as you did with the other strings. Cut off string. Tie one end to the screw-eye on the back of your marionette. Carry it up to the back end of your control marked "back string," pass it up through the slot, wrap it around and pass it through the slot again, as you did before, to insure its not slipping out.

Be sure that the control is always hanging at an even and level keel, so that your marionette has its feet just touching the floor, and that all strings are hanging straight.

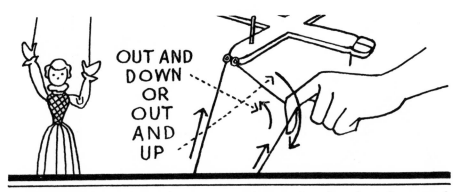

OUT AND
DOWN
OR
OUT
AND
UP

Check all parts to see that your marionette is relaxed, and proceed with the hand strings.

These are also continuous running strings, so measure accordingly. Tie this string to the left hand, which should have a tiny screw-eye already placed, if hands are of wood or, if a hole is drilled, thread the string through at the base of the thumb. Pass string up to control, through both of the screw-eyes on the front part of the control and down to the right hand. Knot securely. Hands should be relaxed at the sides of the marionette.

If movements are needed for the hands to turn in, as a dancer would use them, the knots are placed on the inside of the hand near the center. When you wish hands to turn out, place the knot on the outside, in the middle of the hand. This stringing is for the more awkward characters, such as clowns. Generally the knot should be near the base of the thumb.

Try these various placings of the hand strings, to be sure of the effect. An emergency knot in the case of breakage may be tightened so as to secure it, by placing a drop of glue on knot and allowing it to dry before use.

The last strings to be placed are the leg or foot strings. Tie one end of the strings, after properly measuring them, into each screw-eye, up to each end of the foot-bar, fastening it as above described, for quick changing of strings.

String for foot movement should be long enough for the foot-bar to be placed over the small one inch of doweling on the front of the control, so as to allow the marionette to be always in an upright, relaxed position.

A large darning needle with an eye long enough to carry the string, is necessary to help in this stringing process.

The fastening must be made through the material of the costumes so as to contact the screw-eye which has been placed on the body of your marionette before costuming it. Extra trick strings may be fastened in convenient places on your control with extra screw-eyes or bored holes. A bright bead may identify such extra strings.

A marionette must be costumed before stringing but for diagramatic reasons, they are shown here without costumes, so that the mechanical facts may be made clearer. The three diagrams on the next page describe an exercise called the "Marionette Swing." These motions will help you to become acquainted with your marionettes and familiarize yourself with the different movements.

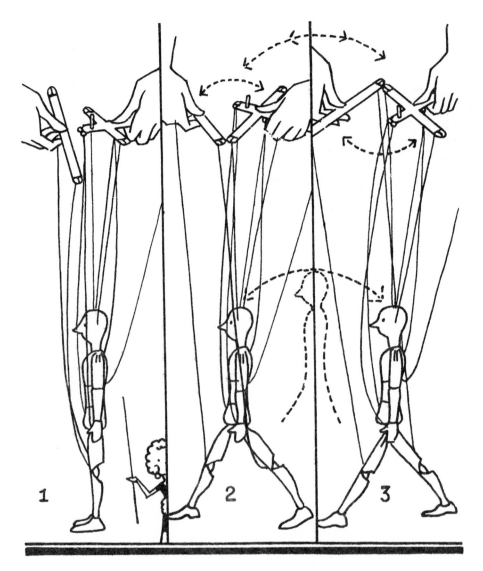

1. The position of the control before starting the marionette swing.

2. First movement.

3. Second movement.

Hold the main part of the control in the left hand and the foot-bar in the right hand. Do not grasp the control too tightly, but be careful not to drop it. This is an unforgivable accident.

1. Kneeling on both knees, hands pleading.

   Lower the marionette to the floor and pull up both hand strings.

2. Kneeling on one knee, one arm raised.

   Pull one arm string, and one foot string.

3. Sitting on chair.

   Bend body forward and lower carefully, then straighten. Place hands.

1. Lifting one hand—by pulling one handstring.

2. Lifting one foot—by tilting the foot-bar.

   Practice alternating left and right arm and hand manipulation.

3. Bowing—by tilting up the back end of the control and pressing the shoulder strings back with the middle finger.

1. Lying on floor or bed.

Relax all strings and lower until the marionette is reclining.

2. Dancing. Try and imitate all hand, foot and body movements of a dancer.

3. Walking on hands. Pull up foot-bar. Lower the marionette carefully so as not to tangle strings. Let head and hands just touch floor. Lift feet high above head. Move across stage in short jumps.

The marionette can reflect all the individualism of the puppeteer which experiment and practice will evolve. The following will depict the fundamental and necessary emotions, gestures and actions that all students should know.

Practice all gestures first with left hand, then with the right.

Head
>Yes.
>No.
>Look to right, then to left.
>Look down.

Hands
>Work one hand alone, then the other hand alone.
>Work both with one hand.
>Work both with continuous string, holding first with right hand, then with the left hand.

Gesture
>"Hello," "Goodbye," "Gimme," "Hands up," first as burglar, then as victim.
>Scratch head.
>Salute.
>Hand to ear.

Walking
>Walk first to right, then to left.
>Walk up, turn around, walk back.
>Walk on, look behind sometimes, walk out.
>Walk up and down steps.
>Cross, first behind, then in front.
>Walk with hand raised.
>Running.

General Body Movements

Bow.

Bow, hand across chest.

Courtesy.

Kneeling, one knee and both knees.

Sitting down and getting up from a chair.

Ditto from floor.

Lying down on floor, then on bed.

Picking object from table.

Picking something from floor.

Climbing.

Pulling and pushing.

Jumping.

Walking on hands.

Emotions

Make up your own words to suit the emotion to be portrayed.

Fright.	Tears.
Anger.	Age.
Excitement.	Fatigue.
Joy.	Sleepiness.
Curiosity.	Stealth.
Laughter.	Shame.

A good method of becoming familiar with the manipulation of your marionette is to repeatedly practice these suggestions until they are a part of the natural handling of your figures; just as a musician must practice the scales in order to become proficient, and to make for perfection.

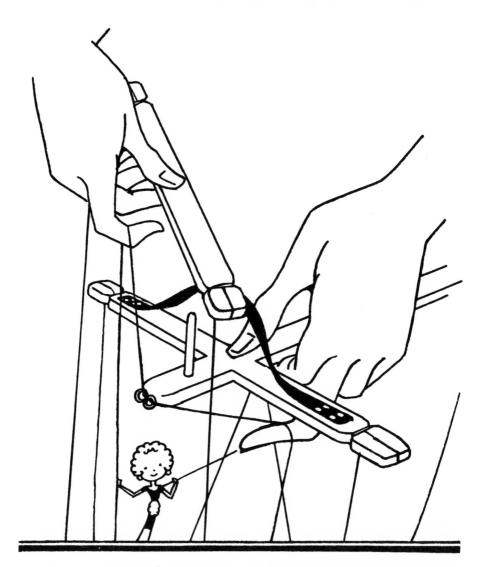

Your control is properly balanced in your hands when you can feel

that the weight may be supported from your middle fingers alone. You

should become so used to your control that the first and little fingers

will be free to pull the different strings. By grasping the footbar

firmly the fingers of the same hand can pull the strings.

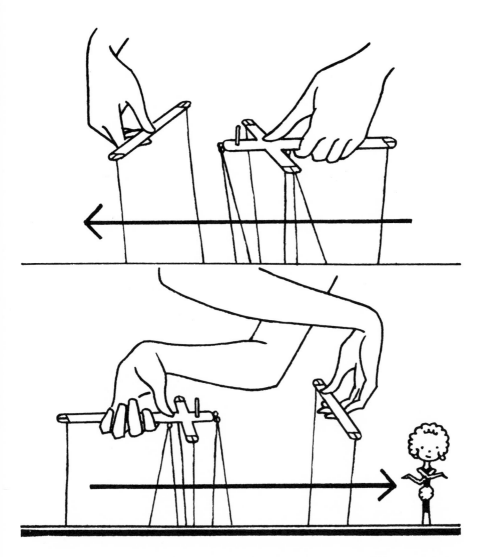

When you wish to turn a marionette around and make him walk the other way, do not clumsily change your control to the other hand, just change the position of your hands and by a slight adjustment of body position, he will continue his movements and steps without interruption. By diligent practice a marionette may be made to face any direction and to make complete turns.

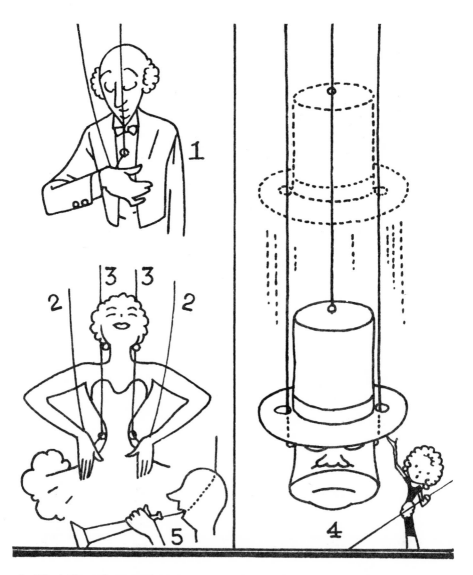

1. To bring the hand up close to the body place a screw-eye on the chest and put the hand string through it.
2. Regular hand strings.
3. Screw-eyes placed at the waist line and an extra string on the hands. Pass the string through these screw-eyes and up to a place on the control bar. Tie these strings together.
4. Method of pulling a hat off of the head.
5. String through head attached to horn or other props to be lifted to the mouth.

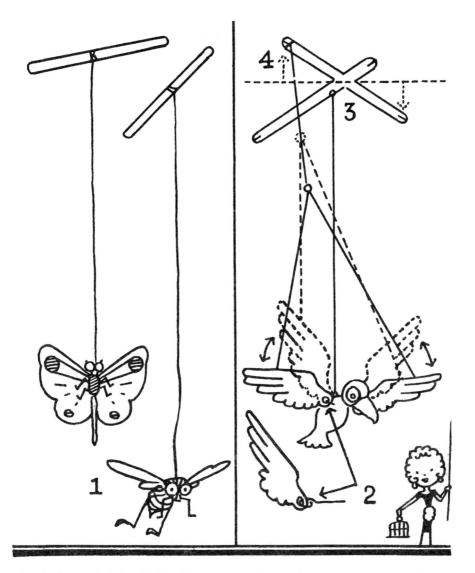

1. A short stick is all that is necessary for an insect, as they just dangle or fly through the air.

   Animals or large birds have a stick control about the length of the animal, with a cross piece if ears, head or wings are to move.

2. Wing fastened loosely with wire loop.

3. Back-string for suspension.

4. Tipping of control for wing movement.

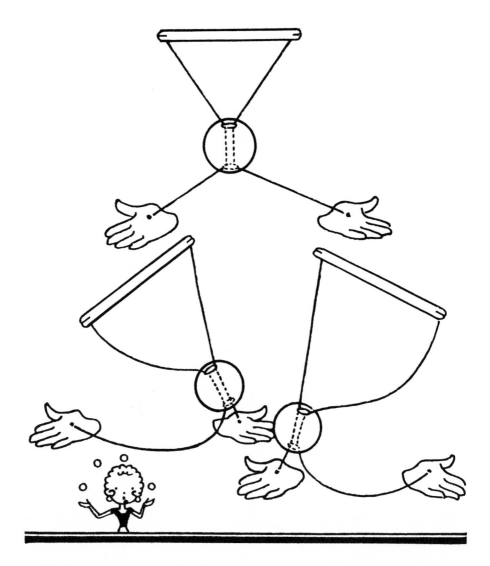

Make a hole in a wooden ball and run both hand strings through it.
Do not fasten to the regular place on the control for the hands. Have
an extra stick about a foot long and tie the hand strings to each end.
As you tip the stick from side to side the ball will be thrown from one
hand to another. See that the palms of the hands are up.

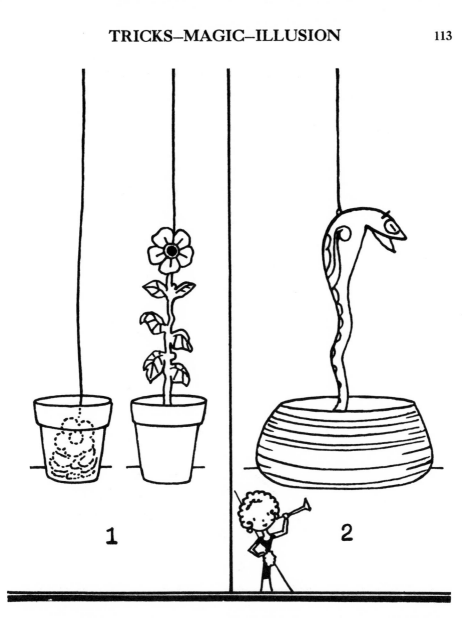

A magical way to make a flower grow from a pot, and a snake to rise from a basket.

1. Make your plant and flower from paper or cloth sewed to a string. Place folded, out of sight in your pot until ready. Pull the string slowly upward and the miracle is performed.

2. A tube of cloth lightly stuffed so it will be very flexible and painted will achieve a terrifying snake.

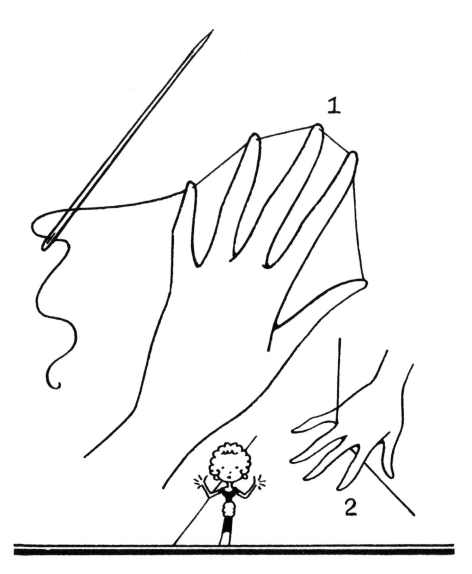

1. The above diagram shows how to prevent the many strings from becoming entangled while manipulating. Use strong thread to attach to the finger ends. With a string guard as in Figure 1 strings will not catch in fingers and prevent manipulation.

2. Here you see how a hand can very easily catch the strings and cause a lot of trouble.

Master Funny-face would like to have the apple he sees at his feet.

1. A tiny screw-eye is placed in the center of his hand and a string passed through it and down to the apple.

2. By lowering the marionette, pulling on the string attached to the apple, and then bringing him back to an erect position, he will lift the apple.

1. A prop treasure chest with a hinged top, with the string attached for lifting.

2. A pirate is opening the chest. Note the hand just touching the lid.

3. The hand string of the marionette and the string of the chest lid are pulled simultaneously.

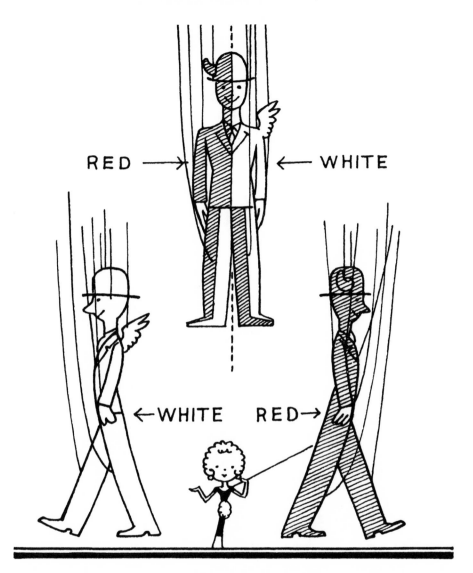

RED →   ← WHITE

←WHITE   RED→

You may wish to experiment with a figure such as is shown above. If each half of your figure is costumed in a different color and manner, it will take on a distinctly different character when it is turned in profile and walked first to the right and then to the left.

Such combinations as angel and devil or any Jekyll and Hyde characters you may think of are always an interesting divertissement.

1. A ghost is composed of a head, a pair of hands and a light transparent cloth.

2. The material is draped loosely over the head shape. The hands are attached to the cloth. Phosphorescent paint will add to the weirdness, as will also a weaving snaky movement of your control

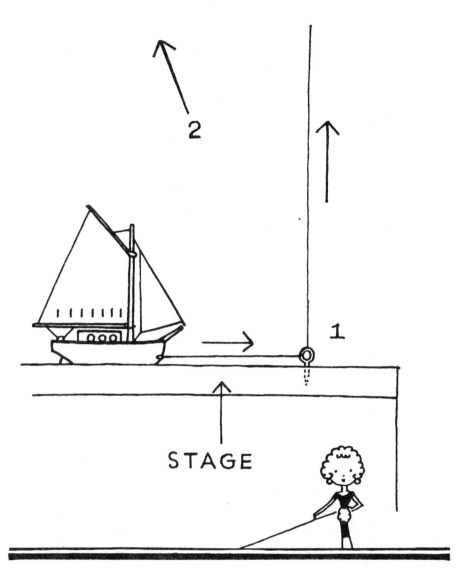

One method of moving props across a stage, such as a ship, house or cart, auto, etc.

1. Place a large screw-eye in the wings of your stage. Attach a string to your prop and pass it through the screw-eye and up to the bridge, where—(2) the operator on the bridge may pull the string.

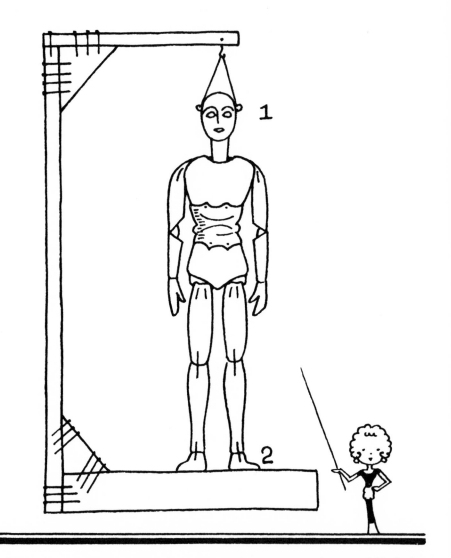

    This is a rack upon which your marionette may hang while being costumed or painted. It may be made of wood or any material you wish, as long as you make it this general shape. The base should be made heavy enough so as not to tip over.

1. Attach a temporary string to the head loops and suspend from a hook in the rack.

2. Allow the feet just to touch the base.

Here is where romance steps in and further rewards the puppeteer for all of his patience and work.

A great help to the costumer is a work rack. Before stringing your marionette, attach a temporary string to the head loops, so that it will hang naturally, with the feet just touching the base. This allows it to be turned and moved about to advantage. This rack may also be used when your marionette is painted.

Costuming a marionette may be as simple or as elaborate as you wish; but there are many things to consider and many things to avoid.

All covering of the joints must allow for freedom of action.

Too many frills may hinder the string movements.

The materials used should be of sufficient strength to withstand wear and tear for use in plays.

The kind of materials used should be confined to the character of the marionette you wish to portray; silk, satin, velvet or chiffon for queens, dancers, fairies and for all of the richer type of costumes. For characters such as peasants, farmers, servants, etc., the use of calicos, muslin, woolens, and cotton goods are in order.

Backgrounds must be considered in your color combinations. Bright colors should be used against dark backgrounds and dark colors against light backgrounds. Jewels and shiny materials reflect the lights of the flood and foot-lights should be used accordingly. Try with research to make the proper type of costume for the character of your marionette.

If a sewing machine is handy, use it, because all seams should be strong. Much of this construction will be done by hand however, and as a marionette gets very rough treatment, this advice remains true: that your costumes must be practical as well as ornamental.

Materials from the family scrap-bag are usually available and the local stores are filled with a wealth of things, which with a joyous discrimination in buying, will answer every need. Jewels, buttons, ribbons, gay handkerchiefs, odds and ends of remnants and small accessories will help you evolve many interesting combinations.

Boots may be added to your marionette by carving them at the same time you make the feet. Joints will not be needed at the ankle as the action will come from the knee. Otherwise the legs and feet may be covered with old kid gloves or oil-cloth.

Discarded old stockings may be used as leg coverings. These are put on before the shoes are constructed.

For characters such as a Russian peasant, the legs and feet may be wrapped in cloth or burlap, always leaving plenty of play in the ankles and knees for free movement.

Hats should not be too large, but if large hats are necessary, a spreader may be used in the stringing to facilitate easier manipulation.

Underclothes are nice addition to your costumes especially if the movements of your marionettes should reveal glimpses of the same. It is interesting to always have in mind the idea that a marionette is a valued work of art and should be treasured as such. You will be proud to display it as such under all circumstances.

While realism may not be the charm of the marionette, the faithfulness of costume detail should be so complete as to include the underclothing, not only as equipment for their action in plays, but to support them at all times as works of art, because of the popular interest in them when on exhibition.

When planning your cast, if a character is to appear in two different costumes, there should be two marionettes constructed just alike because marionettes' clothes cannot be changed quickly enough, on account of the time element for re-stringing purposes.

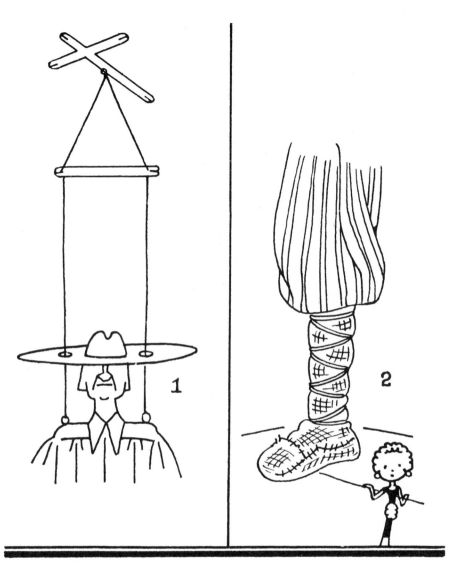

1. Here is shown the method of placing a spreader to widen the space between the strings when large hats are used in the costume.

2. A wrapped burlap covering for a leg belonging to a Russian peasant. A piece of lead for weight is placed on the bottom of the foot before wrapping. Be careful to allow plenty of freedom of movement.

Here we have a very good reason why it is necessary to under-clothe your marionette. Close examination as to details of the costume by your audience is always in order. Under clothing should be finished in detail with the same cared for appearance as outer garments. For comedy effects exaggeration in design and color will produce results.

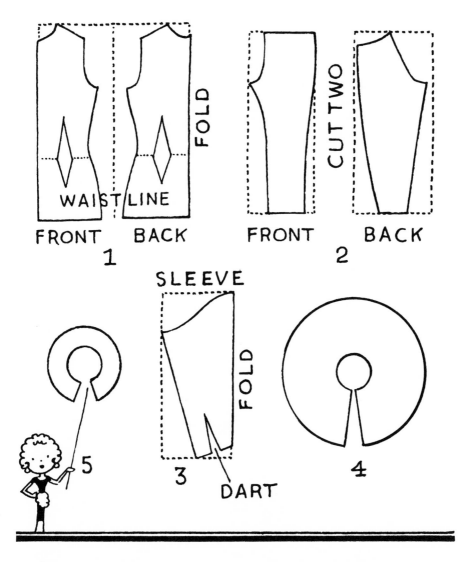

1. Man's waist, fitted or loose. The loose waist is made without the darts. The fitted waist is made with the darts taken in.

2. Man's trouser pattern. Shorten or lengthen as you wish.

3. Loose sleeves made without darts. Fitted use darts.

4. An easy way of cutting a cape.

5. A collar.

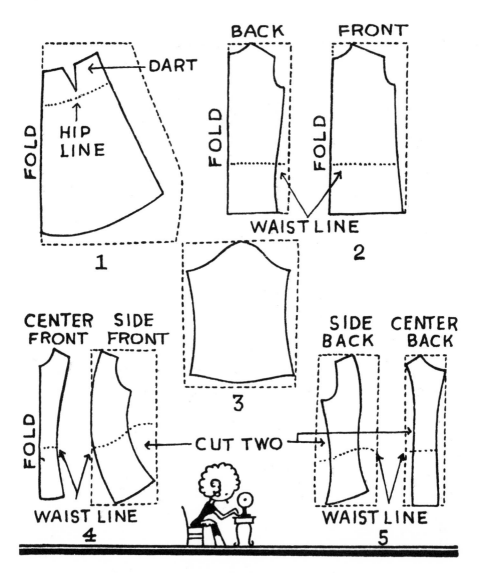

1. Woman's skirt. Use darts for fitting.

2. Woman's loose waist.

3. Woman's loose sleeve. Dart to fit.

4-5. Woman's fitted waist.

These patterns are basic. Your own ingenuity will evolve variations and inventions of your own.

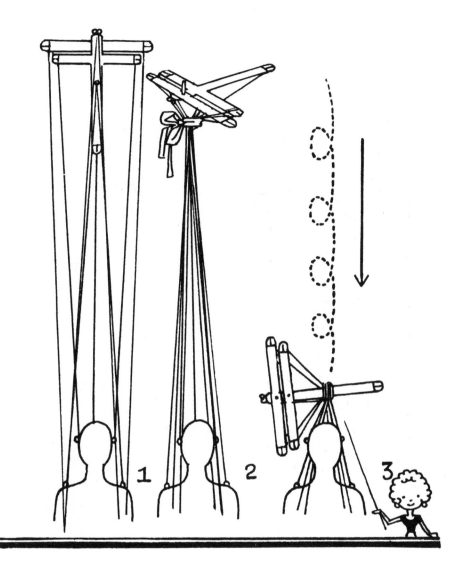

1. Finished marionette, strung, costumed and ready to be placed in its own bag.

2. A piece of tape tied around the strings near the control, pushed up firmly. This will hold the foot-bar in place.

3. Now wrap the strings around your control, leaving several inches of the string free.

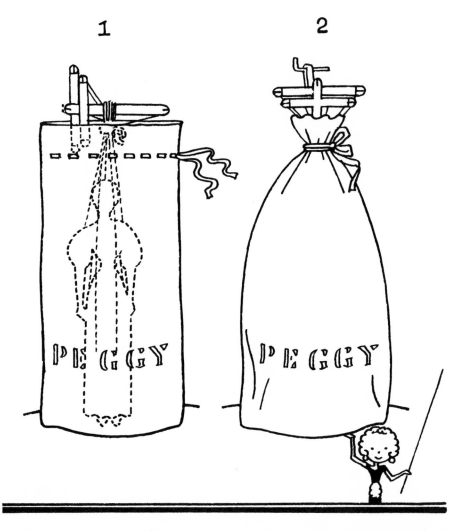

1. Have your bag ready with the name of your marionette on the bag.

Lower your marionette into the bag. Allow plenty of room so as not to crowd or disarrange the costume.

2. Place back end of the control in the bag. Draw the string and tie the string around the control. Hang up by the strap on the control.

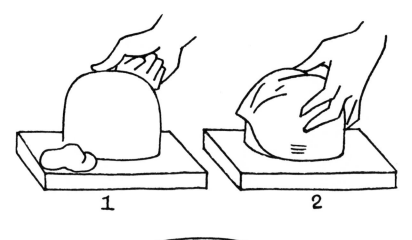

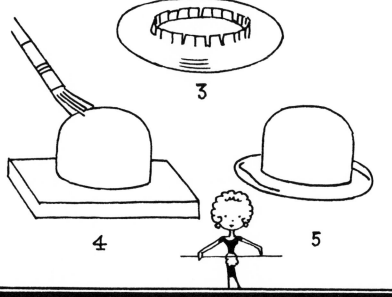

1. Model the crown of the hat with plastelline.

2. Dampened buckram pressed and smoothed to shape over your model.

3. Cut a piece of buckram or stiff felt for the hat brim.

4. Cover well with thick glue.

5. When completely dry and stiff, sew or glue parts together and paint. Put on a band.

Nelly the Nag is only a marionette mare, but she is a faithful friend to her master, the Cop. She is gentle and for a few lumps of sugar will do many tricks, and is anxious to tell you in her own way that she is still too young to vote.

An animal marionette may be made of any material that resembles the animal you wish to make—cloth, fur, leather, plush, etc.

Make a pattern in the general shape of the animal you desire. A good way is to find a picture of said animal to be sure of the correctness of every detail.

The neck should be left unstuffed and the body stuffed loosely.

The head may be made the same way as the other marionette heads.

The bodies may be made of paper mache.

An inside construction of wood or cardboard will help hold out the body, with the contour and shape stuffed out with cotton. Sometimes sticks inside of the cloth legs will stiffen them. Always weight the feet well.

Legs may be attached by wire run through the body, or else by chamois or leather hinges. The legs must swing easily.

Use shoe buttons or beads for the eyes.

The tails may be made of unraveled rope-yarn.

Animals are funnier if not too realistic, but can be made as **flexible** as you wish by following the details described regarding **the human** marionettes.

Here is a view of a boy trying out his finished marionette. Notice the position of his hands and the relation of the control to the strings on the marionette.

Br-r-r-r-r. What a night when black cats, ghosts and weird hob-goblins go hooting through space. Any audience would need but one guess to know that this is Old Mother Witch herself. So beware, she will cast a spell upon you.

Lulu, the Hula maid. She has "it" and never is so real as when a phonograph is playing Hawaiian music. Visions of the beach at Waikiki and moonlight nights in Hawaii will be yours if you use a back drop of palms and sandy beach.

Floppo, the Clown is the champion roller skater of Puppet Land. With his hands fastened behind his back and a nice smooth floor to skate on, he will glide about and do many surprising bits of plain and fancy skating.

Ivanichkey, the marvelous Russian Kosatski dancer. This is his pose when not doing one of his famous holoopas. It will give any puppeteer a thrill to make him do his intricate dances.

You may thank your lucky stars you do not look like this gazer of the skies, but he shows how caricature may add to a marionette.

By careful modeling an almost real appearance of individuals may be achieved, and with the correct detail of costume, portray them like an oil painting.

Production
and Stagecraft

A marionette rack on which you may hang your marionettes by the leather strap of the control when not in use.

2″ x ⅞″ furring will be ample for the necessary strength for this rack.

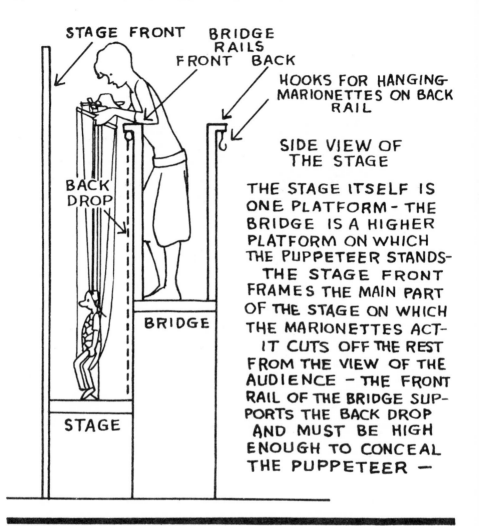

STAGE FRONT   BRIDGE
RAILS
FRONT   BACK

HOOKS FOR HANGING
MARIONETTES ON BACK
RAIL

BACK
DROP

SIDE VIEW OF
THE STAGE

THE STAGE ITSELF IS
ONE PLATFORM - THE
BRIDGE IS A HIGHER
PLATFORM ON WHICH
THE PUPPETEER STANDS-
THE STAGE FRONT
FRAMES THE MAIN PART
OF THE STAGE ON WHICH
THE MARIONETTES ACT-
IT CUTS OFF THE REST
FROM THE VIEW OF THE
AUDIENCE - THE FRONT
RAIL OF THE BRIDGE SUP-
PORTS THE BACK DROP
AND MUST BE HIGH
ENOUGH TO CONCEAL
THE PUPPETEER —

BRIDGE

STAGE

The staging of a marionette show will bring you the thrill and experience of professional producers, because it calls into use all the arts of the theatre and stage and many others.

A marionette stage consists of the following:

A stage front which conceals the puppeteers.

Openings at front, sides and below stage.

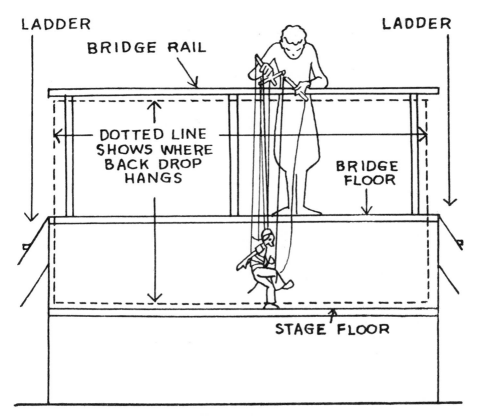

LADDER   LADDER

BRIDGE RAIL

DOTTED LINE
SHOWS WHERE
BACK DROP
HANGS

BRIDGE
FLOOR

STAGE FLOOR

THE STAGE
SHOWN WITH THE STAGE FRONT
REMOVED

The proscenium opening in the stage front.

A curtain just behind the stage front, which closes to shut off the proscenium opening.

A bridge or platform just behind the stage, somewhat higher than the stage level on which the puppeteers stand.

Ladders or steps for entry and exit to stage bridge.

TEASER OR TOP MASKING PIECE

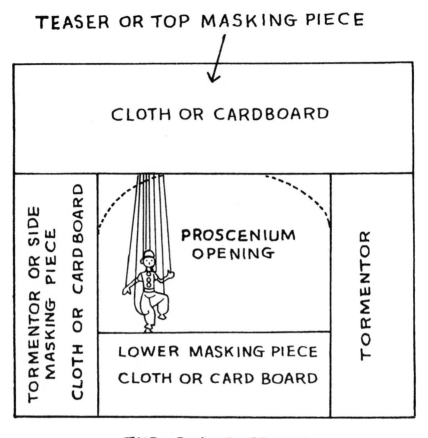

THE STAGE FRONT
MADE OF DRAPES SCREENS ETC

A bridge rail at the front of the bridge over which the puppeteers lean, and which supports the back drops.

A rail at the back of the bridge from which the marionettes are hung when not in use.

Ladders or steps at each side, or the end of the bridge, to provide easy access to the bridge.

It is not always necessary to build a stage like the one described in the pictures in order to enjoy your marionettes. A convenient doorway with kitchen tables, a bench, and curtains may be used. A piece of compo-board with the arch cut out will serve for your proscenium front.

Back drop and drapes will hide puppeteers from the audience.

While some may prefer the up and down type of curtain which rolls up like a window shade, the draw-curtain is the most popular. This style of curtain is hung from rings which are sewed into the curtain, six inches apart, and which slide back and forth upon a wire. This wire is stretched taut with turnbuckles, or with wingnuts, on the eye-bolts to which the ends are attached.

The two halves of the curtain should overlap at least six inches to a foot when the curtain is closed, so it is necessary to have a separate wire for each half of your curtain. Simple draw curtain rigging may be bought at the upholsterers. Sketch shows the details of the curtain stringing which you may make yourself.

Marionettes usually make their entrances and exits from the sides or wings of the stage, so this space must be left clear overhead, as well as on the stage at all times. However, the use of a trap-door in stage floor, a fire-place or other props to conceal the marionettes, may be used for your entrance and exit. Just remember the possible catching of the strings and the upsetting of props or other marionettes and never overcrowd your stage floor.

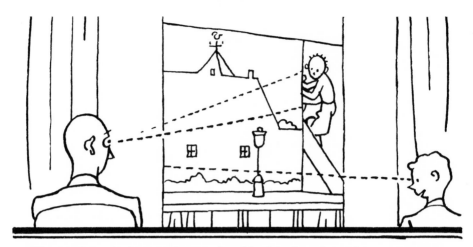

Use a plain dark curtain, preferably black velvet, for a permanent back drop, as this makes the strings less conspicuous, and will mask operations back stage.

This curtain should hang from the bridge rail with rings and hooks. The curtain material should be made of a heavy grade of goods, as skimpy drapes are apt to be transparent, and show shadows of the operator.

Upright flat pieces are sometimes used at either side of the stage to conceal off-stage space, but room must be left for curtain and for marionettes to enter and exit freely. Enough room must also be left for figures to pass in entry or exit.

The border is a strip hung across the top of the front of the stage to conceal bridge-rail and heads and hand of puppeteers, and also to conceal stage near floor.

Some thought must be given to using your skill as a scenic artist and ways to transpose and enlarge pictures to your scenery. You can make use of the method of employing the enlarging squares, but here are a number of suggestions and things to do to help you.

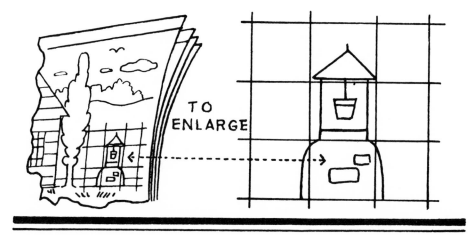

Procure pictures of the objects you want to include in your back-drop scene, clipped from magazines, etc. Rule small squares over it. Rule squares on your scene as many times larger as you want the object to show and then proceed with the suggestions below.

Procure a piece of unbleached muslin the size of your stage back.

Have design ready beforehand.

Outline everything with ordinary black wax crayon.

This wax crayon outline will help keep your colors from running or spreading.

Obtain color inks of colors wanted, and a tube of flat white water color.

Have containers ready. Quart size bottles or containers are ideal, as enough color should be mixed before starting, to cover all surfaces with each color selected for use.

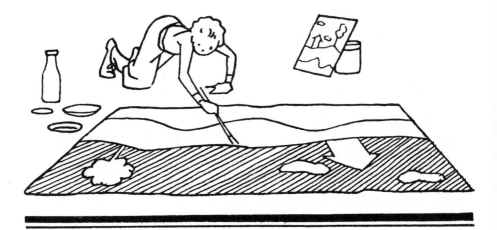

Fill bottle or container almost full of water. Put in a small quantity of ink at a time until color is of the required shade or tint.

From the tube of flat white water color squeeze in about half a teaspoonful to a quart.

This is to make the tint slightly opaque.

Then get a piece of soap and with a wet brush rub it on the cake of soap and stir enough soap into the mixture with the brush to bring bubbles to the surface.

This acts as a binder and will make the colors go on evenly, smoothly and flat, without globules of moisture. Experiment on a small piece of cloth first.

Now place newspapers under your muslin to absorb any color which might go through. This should dry overnight if color is used carefully and painted on quickly.

Do not paint over the wax lines.

The muslin may be tacked on to wood strips at the top and bottom and fastened to the rail at the back of stage.

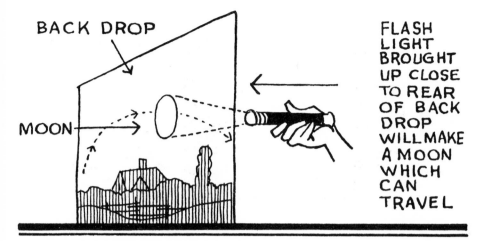

BACK DROP

MOON

FLASH LIGHT BROUGHT UP CLOSE TO REAR OF BACK DROP WILL MAKE A MOON WHICH CAN TRAVEL

The process of lighting your stage is very important. Strip lights and spot lights are fine if you can obtain them. Failing this, a row of lights across the front of the stage high enough to illuminate to the floor can be used. However, footlights should be the basis for your lighting. Several strings of Christmas tree lights can be used as footlights.

A flash light held behind and directly against the back drop with corresponding blue lights in your foots will give an excellent moonlight effect.

A separate or extra string of blue bulbs in your footlights will be found useful in producing weird, mysterious and ghost effects.

Another arrangement is a single small reflector, or even a single bulb, on either side of the opening just behind the stage front and strung so as not to interfere with the marionette movements. Small fluted tins to be found in the 10¢ store provide splendid reflectors. Spots or floods on stands are good, but be careful to place them out of the line of vision of the audience.

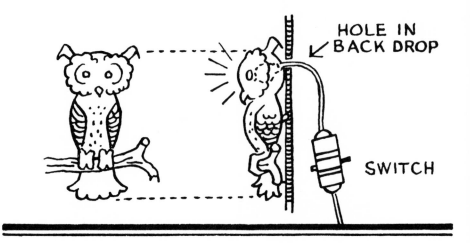

Choose one or all of these methods and experiment.

You can create a number of effects with tiny lights, such as eyes in the dark, light fixtures on the stage, lamp posts, etc., not forgetting the old reliable flash-light of many uses.

Sometimes it is quite dark back stage, so a light on the hanging rail in order to see your marionettes and for possible repairs or untangling is useful. This should be shaded from the view of the audience

The arrangements for controlling your lights may be anything from a simple 3-way socket to a complicated set of switches and dimmers. With colored cellophane many different effects may be obtained. The cellophane can be cemented to cardboard frames and placed over footlights or floods. Leave a space of two inches or more between bulb and cellophane frame so heat from the bulb will not destroy it.

Various attachments, plugs, sockets and switches for extensions and wiring for your light effects can be procured in the ten cent store.

"Props" is the word used to designate the articles you use on your stage, such as furniture, accessories, and possible mechanical arrangements to complete your show. These may be built of wood, paper-mache, or any material you think suitable. Upholstered and painted small articles may be bought at various places. Always be sure in your selection that they are true to the scale of your marionettes and stage.

The proportion of props should be true to the size or scale of your marionette figures. You can check this by the comparison of objects in normal use, that is, a chair is knee high to your figure—a table, a little below waist high.

The smaller props sometimes needed may include a toy telephone, dishes, window curtains, cupboard, toy plants in pots, framed pictures to hang or painted on back drops, baskets and utensils of various kinds.

A list of small props which may be used many times over is as follows: Chair, table, steps, tree-stumps.

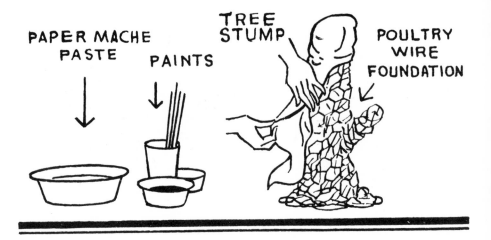

PAPER MACHE PASTE

PAINTS

TREE STUMP

POULTRY WIRE FOUNDATION

A good method of building tree trunks, stumps, lamp-posts, rocks, etc., is to have paper-mache mixture in a pail in sufficient quantity to allow for dipping pieces of cloth into it. This, when well soaked with the mixture, may be placed or wrapped around a foundation built of wire or wood, and the result when dry and painted will be very realistic. Chairs and tables must be sufficiently weighted so as not to be overturned. Be careful not to have edges or extra trimming to catch the strings. It is better to use paint to decorate with than other ornamentation.

Props for your play should be kept in groups for each scene and put in a handy place back stage so as to be ready for the acts in order of their use.

One person really should be put in charge of the props and the care of them. That and the opening and closing of the curtain should be his important and entire job.

This fellow's name is usually "Props."

Of all the arts to be found in puppeteering, music surely is not the least. It makes all the other arts come to life and have a meaning the human heart can understand. Rhythm or tempo is the indispensable thing that pulls and holds all the other elements of your show together, producing the effect of realism.

This brings us to the importance of sound effects in the production of your marionette show. A list of instruments, any one of which with a little practice may be mastered, can be introduced into your production at the proper time. For instance, if you have a marionette playing the piano, a person behind the scenery will play the music. A small toy piano may be procured or even built for a stage prop.

A victrola may be used as entertainment or to hold attention, before the curtain goes up, during the intermissions, and for the finale. If an old-time music box is available it is an invaluable help because of its character of tinkly tunes which are so appropriate. Perhaps someone can play the accordion, harmonica or some other instrument. The marionette on the stage should be provided with a corresponding instrument in miniature.

Many things may be introduced to help out for sound effects, such as:

Jew's harp
Harmonica
Hand Bell
Bicycle Bell (may be used for a phone ring)
Castanets ⎫
Tambourine ⎬ for dancers
Musical Gongs (good for use just before curtain rises)
Drums or Tom-toms
Whistles (bird notes)
Cocoanuts halves (used for hoof beats of horses)
Kazoo (ghost effects)
Flat thin board on string swinging around (wind)
Sheet of tin and flash light (thunder and lightning)
Peas or beans falling in wooden box (rain)

Tin can with string through bottom—rosin on string (makes a raucous noise)

Besides the mechanical noises, some practice should be given to rehearsing noises such as coughs, sneezes, yawning, laughing, crying, shrieks, barking of dogs, growling of bears, roaring of lions, mooing of cows, grunt of a hog or pig squeal, and many others you may add to your repertoire.

Even though you have prepared your show with the utmost care, something always happens; a string breaks; a knee joint cracks up; a prop is broken in transit. Carry with you a box or a bag containing everything in the way of tools and materials that you might possibly need to make repairs. Take a small amount of each.

Here is a partial list which you should add to as your needs call for.

Hammer	Tacks
Pliers	Wire, light and heavy
Screw Driver	Nails, several sizes
Drill	Screw eyes, assorted
Scissors	Stringing cord
Knife	Heavy string
Electric Connection	Glue
Extra light bulbs	Extra shoes or feet
Pins, straight and safety	Muslin
Paint and brushes	Trunk fibre
Needle and thread	Weighting lead

Stringing needle (darning)

Do not forget to make use of a phenomenon that never fails to make an impression on your audience. After the show is over and before the room is lighted, step down on your stage out in front of your back drop with a marionette. The marionette shown becomes so lifelike after the audience has been concentrating on the play, and the sense of scale has so warped down, that any part of a human suddenly seen with a marionette, for a moment, appears like a giant in comparison and you will always hear the audience gasp.

A definite procedure should be followed in producing a play which will alleviate embarrassment and build to a perfect performance.

First set up your stage and have everything ready hours before your show is to be given—drapes, curtains, lights, etc. Long before the performance is to start have your marionettes on the rail in position for their entrances.

Props and scenery should be back stage.

First set should be in position on the stage.

Puppeteers should all be accounted for.

Check on strings and details of costumes, props, etc.

This regular procedure is a good thing to keep in mind throughout the performance.

1. Foots up.
2. House lights out.
3. Open curtain.
4. Announcer, if one is used.
5. Announcer appears before curtain opens.
6. First act.
7. Curtain closed on cue.
8. Shift set of lights if necessary.
9. Foots remain up on curtain.
10. Second act and repeat.
11. Final curtain.
12. House lights up.

CONDUCT SOUND EFFECTS

First select your play.

Prepare all advertising, tickets and programs.

If your selection of a play entails permission from the author, do this, otherwise you may have to pay for royalties.

Your program should contain these items. Name of Play. Name of Author. Time and Place. Names of marionette characters. Names of Puppeteers, Director and Ticket Seller.

There are any number of marionette plays available from books that have been written by famous puppeteers, and are to be found in the Public Libraries all over the United States and other countries. The play prepared for you in this book is a sample of the type of play for beginners. Try your hand at writing your own play. Fairy tales make good material from which to make a play, but take into consideration the special requirements of action or ideas of action, and not too much dialogue. Situations where something happens all the time, with few long speeches are best.

TO ACCOMODATE BACK ROW OF THE AUDIENCE

There are certain things that a marionette can do that the human actor cannot, and visa versa. Tricks done by an actor have little interest, but will arouse great enthusiasm and admiration when done by a marionette. These tricks are basically simple, and the use of them will provide the humor and gaiety which is the real mission of the marionette show. Clear, distinct enunciation is of utmost importance, always remembering that it is not the loudness of the voice that will reach the back row of the audience, but the clearness, timing, and sureness of your enunciation and the absolute letter perfectness of what you wish conveyed to your audience that counts.

It is always a good idea to have an understudy for every part, so you will never be at a loss when giving your show. One of the things to remember is that when a marionette is supposed to be speaking, that is the one that shows the arm action. The other marionettes on the stage should show, by their inaction and quietness that they are listening, so as not to draw attention from the speaker. Stage waits are to be avoided. If through some unlooked for incident a break or stage wait seems unavoidable, fill in the pause with impromptu action and speech until the regular script action and dialogue can be picked up and continued.

CHARACTERS

The Maid.
The Prince.
The Witch.
The Parrot.
The Dove.
The Tree.
Birds, Butterflies, Turtle, White Rabbit.

IN THREE ACTS

Act 1. Scene 1—A room in the old witch's cottage.
Act 2. Scene 1—In the Wood.
Act 3. Scene 1—In the Wood.

ACT 1

Scene 1—A room in the old witch's cottage. The witch is discovered leaning over the fire and muttering. A parrot is in a cage. A table and a stool.

Witch—"Heh! Heh! Heh! Three score and more. They all were men but now they're trees. Three score and ten."

Parrot—(Shrieks. The witch goes over to the cage.)

Parrot—"Ha-a-a-a-ark!"

Witch—"Heh! Heh! Heh! 'Tis three score years and ten that they have stood there, but they'll be there for all eternity. Each and every one of them are in my power. Ye-a-ah. A Prince and his whole army changed into trees and the spell shall be kept upon them forever and ever. (Witch addresses bird) So-o-o-o-o, my pretty bird, don't you dare to let that magic ring get away from you. So long as you guard it with your life, a prince and his servants shall remain as trees. So long as you hold it tight, there's crackers for you. But so long as you don't hold the ring tight, you'll be bird-porridge for me. It is my will!"

(Knock on the door.)

Witch—"What's that? Who's there?"

Parrot—(Shrieks) "Ha-a-a-ark."

(The maid enters.)

Witch—"Well, come in, come in." (impatiently. When witch sees girl, changes her voice to tone of sugary sweetness.)

"Oh, a good morning, my child. 'Tis a rare day indeed that I have a visitor and one so sweet besides. Who are you?"

Maid—"Alas, may it please you, it matters not so much who I am. Far more important is my quest."

Witch—"Eh! Your quest? Your quest indeed! And what may that be?"

Parrot—(Squawks, and the ring falls.)

Maid—"See! there's my quest. I have been bidden to fetch that ring to its rightful owner."

Witch—(Angrily) "Do not touch it—go away! Touch it at your peril! Go way!" (Girl picks up the ring—the witch tries to grab the girl, who gets away from her, and gets out after a struggle.)

Witch—(To parrot as girl exits) "So you faithless bird. Curses upon you, that you should betray me and let her have the ring. Take that and that." (Witch beating the bird, continues to berate it.) "I'll pull me a wish with your wish bone, you green devil bird. Take that!" (Thunder and lightning mingled with shrieks of Witch and Parrot as the curtain falls.)

ACT 2

Scene 1—In the Wood—Large tree with movable (arms) branches, at right center. Tree stump at right. Butterflies, Rabbit, Frog and Turtle. The scene opens on a peaceful wood scene. There are bird sounds; butterflies are flitting about; the frog is hopping about, and the rabbit jumps off the tree stump and scurries across the stage; the turtle walks slowly away, and then a white dove flies in.

White Dove—"Coo-oo-ooo." (Voice of maid offstage) "Alright little white dove."

White Dove—"Coo-oo-ooo." (Girl's voice still offstage) "Yes— I'm coming—I'm coming."

White Dove—"Coo-oo Coo-oo-ooo Co-o-o-coo." (The girl enters.)

Maid—"Here I am, little white dove. My! How impatient you are! You know a little girl like me can't walk as fast as you can fly."

White Dove—Coo-oo-ooo.

Maid—"What is that you say? (Sits on a tree stump).

White Dove—Coo-oo-ooo-coo.

Maid—"Oh yes—here is the ring you asked me to get from the old woman in the wood. My, what a time I had getting it, but here it is. Oh! (gets up and walks over to tree.) And here is the tree you wanted me to bring it to. Oh, what a grand big beautiful tree it is."

White Dove—(With a triumphant coo—flies up and out.)

Maid—"Oh dear, he's gone. (Calls for dove and looks about.) "Little white dove, where are you? Why did you leave me? Now what shall I do? Here is the tree he told me to wait under, and here is the magic ring. Oh dear, I wonder what it is all about." (She leans against the tree trunk and waits.) (The tree arms begin to move downward slowly. The girl looks up startled.)

Maid—*"Oh, what is that?"* (Arms of tree move closer.) *"Why how strange!* Oh! Oh, dear." (Starts to cry.)

Tree—"Be not afraid———Let me embrace you with boundless thanks for what you have done."

Maid—"Who—who is speaking? Who are you?"

Tree—"Ah, you will be surprised! I am as young as even you are, and I am a Prince indeed."

Maid—"A Prince! But all I can see is a tree."

Tree—"Even so—I am a Prince, and soon you shall see. But first, let me thank you as I want to for what you have done." (Arms of tree slowly embrace girl.)

CURTAIN

ACT 3

Scene 1—Same as Act 2. In the Wood. Large tree is now changed to half man—half tree. The upper part of the large tree now appears as the Prince with his arms about the girl, in the same position as in Act 2.

Maid—"Oh—oh—what———" (Steps away from Prince's embrace.)

Prince—"Now—do you see the Prince? How good it is to be nearly a man again."

Maid—"But why were you a tree, if you are truly a Prince?"

Prince—"Long, long ago, I was enchanted by the old woman in the wood. She turned me into the tree, even as she did all my men and horses. See they are all about us, and soon, thanks to you, my lovely one, they too shall be returned to the world of action again."

Maid—"Oh my Prince, didn't you get tired of being in one place so long?"

Prince—"Oh yes indeed, but now that is all over. How glad I am that my age was suspended, so that I could stay young until you came to this world, and now I know you. Think of it. Always a tree, except for two hours each day, when I was a dove. And when I flew to you and asked a favor for love, you rescued the ring from the old woman in the wood, and thus you broke the enchantment."

Maid—"Oh! Now I understand, and I am so glad to have been a help to you."

Prince—"I shall be eternally grateful to you—and now I want to make you my bride and take you away to my castle, where you shall live happily for evermore." (The tree opens and the Prince steps out, and kneels in front of the girl.)

Prince—"Think not my sweet——that I do this as a payment of a debt. Your charm and kindly heart have made me your slave and for your own dear self alone, I ask you to be my future queen."

Maid—"Oh, my Prince, I accept. I will go with you."

Prince—"This golden magic ring which you rescued from the old woman in the wood shall be our troth. Little did you know when you were procuring this ring and guarding it so carefully, that it was to be your wedding ring."

Maid—"Oh, how beautiful it is."

(Bugle call off stage.)

Prince—"Hark! Hear the bugle call as all my escorts change to men again after being trees. See them all—see they are falling in line. So come, my darling——we will lead the procession into my father's kingdom."

(The Prince and Maid walk off stage as the curtain closes.)

CURTAIN

THE WITCH

THE MAID

THE PRINCE

THE ANIMALS

THE TRANSFORMATION

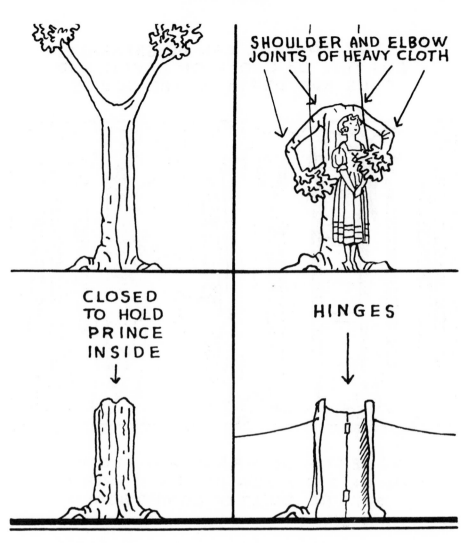

1—The enchanted tree as it appears in scene—the control strings are attached to the two branches.

2—The arms of the enchanted tree as they embrace the maid. (Closing of scene Act 2.)

3—The enchanted tree in which the Prince is standing. (Opening scene Act 3.)

4—The method of releasing the Prince showing hinges and control strings to open tree—to release Prince.

TOP FOLIAGE CAN BE SEPARATE.
CUT OUT OF CLOTH OR PAPER AND
THUS ADD DEPTH TO THE SCENE

SILHOUETTE OF GRASS AND FLOWERS
CAN BE SET A FEW INCHES IN FRONT -
MAY BE BUILT OF COMPO BOARD -

Above is a back drop design for the woods which may be enlarged as explained earlier in the book.

On the stage complete the scene with the enchanted tree which was explained on Page 173—Tree Stump, Butterflies, Rabbit, Frog and Turtle.

The effect of a quiet peaceful wood scene can be enhanced through the use of soft yellow lights in footlights or spots.

COB WEBS CAN BE EFFECTED
BY DRAPING AND PAINTING
CHEESE CLOTH OR PAPER

PROPS MAY BE EITHER
PAINTED OR BUILT AND ATTACHED

Above is a backdrop design for the interior of the witch's cottage which may be enlarged as explained earlier in the book.

On the stage, complete the scene with a table, a chair and a parrot stand.

Plan the backdrop coloring and furniture to have a gloomy suggestion in keeping with a witch's home, and to contrast with the brighter colors of the actor's costumes, such as the girl and the parrot.

Blue floods used in this scene will be most effective, as they give a weird and gloomy effect.

IF CLOUDS ARE COTTON BATTING
PASTED ONTO BACKDROP A REALISTIC
ATMOSPHERIC EFFECT MAY BE MADE

LOWER STRIP OF GRASS AND EVEN
THE FENCE CAN BE SEPARATE AND
THUS ADD MUCH DEPTH -

The back drop must not compete too much with the colors of your props, and the costumes of the marionettes.

Keep them in neutral tones. If a dark drop is used, with black strings on the marionettes, the strings will become almost invisible, and your audience will forget the strings are being pulled.

Grey strings are preferable for light drops, and in fact for all purposes.

LAMP MAY BE CUT OUT AND LIT
FROM BEHIND THE BACKDROP

VINE CAN BE PAINTED OR MADE
OF ROPE AND ARTIFICIAL LEAVES
SEWED ON

To plant the illusion of a city location, avoid scenes too much involved with perspectives and small detail. The broader and more simple a backdrop can be made, the more vital is the interest in the action of the play. Resort to walls, door ways, park benches and symbols associated with the city to give the effect.

Remember the suggestion regarding the use of neutral colors, for vivid or bright color will distract audience attention from the performing marionettes. Of course, do not go to extreme drab color treatment of greys, black and browns—use all colors, but in soft neutral tones.

KEEP GENERAL COLOR EFFECT
IN A PASTEL KEY

MAKE SKY BLUE — HILL TO BE A
PALE OLIVE GREEN — GRASSES AND
FOLIAGE TO BE A DARKER BLUE GREEN

For an opening four feet by seven feet, fifteen yards of material is needed.

This amount allows for a fifty percent fullness. If the material used is of a thin texture, a lining will be needed.

Velvet or heavy material that does not allow the light to shine through is recommended.

USE STRONG BRIGHT COLORS FOR
SMALL ACCENTS SUCH AS CLOTHING
OF GNOMES FLOWERS AND MUSHROOMS

EMERALD GREEN FROG AND CANDY-
SNAPPER - SPIDER CAN BE BUILT
AND STRUNG SO AS TO SWAY WITH CURTAIN

A curtain for a marionette show should be gay and happy, even whimsical. This not only will intrigue your audience, and arouse an air of expectation while they are waiting for the show to begin, but you will carry on a tradition of make-believe so dear to the hearts of both children and grown-ups. However, if this is not possible, a plain colored curtain will answer your purpose.

KEEP THE BACKGROUND TINTS IN

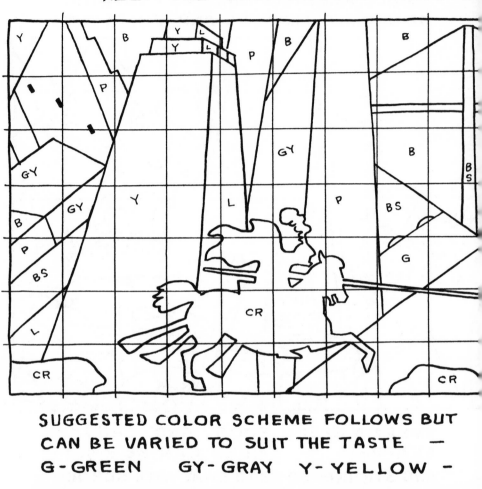

SUGGESTED COLOR SCHEME FOLLOWS BUT CAN BE VARIED TO SUIT THE TASTE — G-GREEN GY-GRAY Y-YELLOW –

The above is a good example of a method of design for a curtain or a backdrop. It could be accomplished with flat masses and silhouettes, and gives color variety a full chance, free from detail distraction, and thus makes decoration the primary purpose and final effect.

ЭNOTONE AND A BALANCED EVEN EFFECT

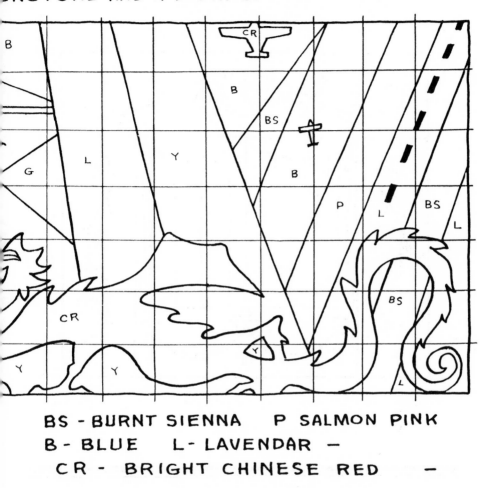

BS - BURNT SIENNA   P SALMON PINK
B - BLUE   L - LAVENDAR —
CR - BRIGHT CHINESE RED   —

In the case of a backdrop, extreme simplicity gives a complete impression, and leaves the wealth of detail of the scene to be found in the marionettes and their props.

The flats and silhouettes are easily made by persons whose artistic abilities are limited.

The stage frontings may be plain if the materials used are rich, and have fabric appeal. Otherwise there are two basic treatments recommended. One is a decorative and interesting curtain leaving the teaser, tormentors, and masking pieces plain. If the curtain is plain, then make the surrounding pieces ornamented. The more or less conventional decoration will wear well.

Try not to have your hands much below the rail because they may be seen by your audience, and spoil the show. Here is one place to consider the other fellow. Each puppeteer must at all times keep track of what the other puppeteers are doing, in order to avoid interfering with them, while at the same time he is accomplishing his own work. Co-operation is the key to a successful performance.

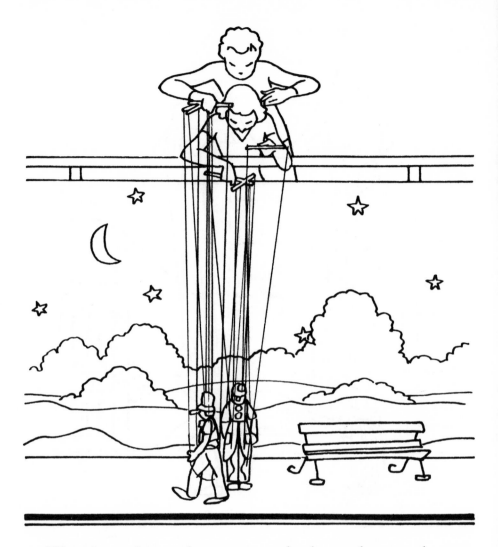

When the marionettes have to pass each other on the stage, the same thing has to happen up on the bridge. Here is where the play can make the wrong kind of hit. This function should be practiced repeatedly until perfected by the puppeteers, so that they feel confident upon the occasion of its use. Again be reminded never to let the control get away from you.

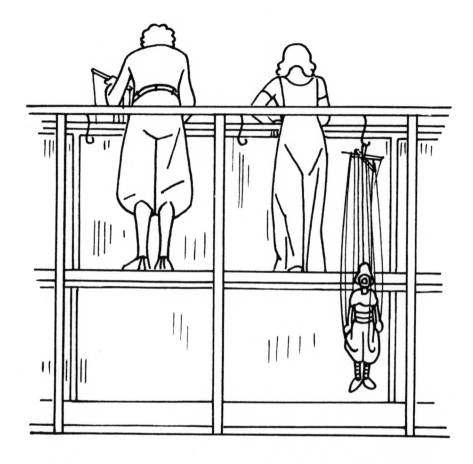

The above illustration will convince you that the puppeteers should wear clothing that is comfortable for them and of the practical sort to avoid entanglements. Pajama suits or overalls for girls are suggested as skirts interfere. Soft shoes or sneakers avoid foot scraping sounds.

Use the elbow support on the rail to maintain comfort when performing.